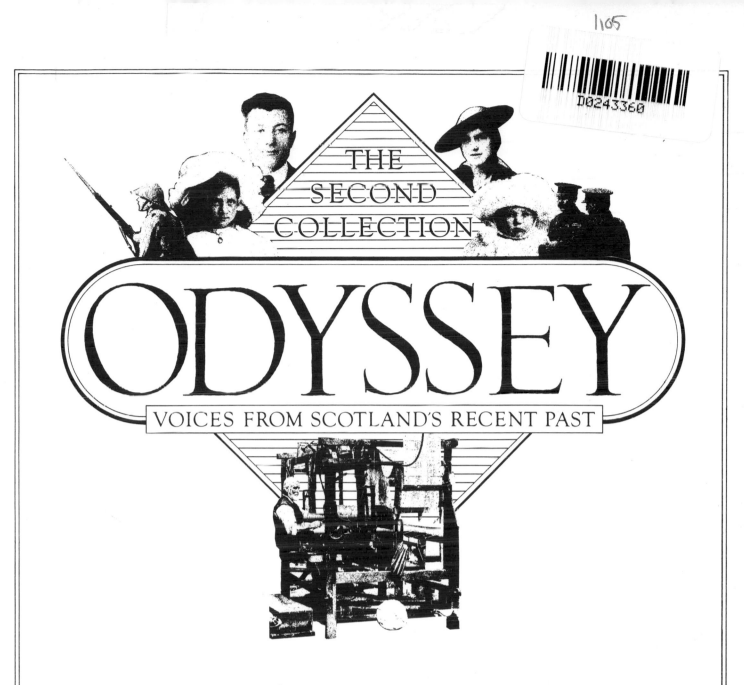

THE SECOND COLLECTION

ODYSSEY

VOICES FROM SCOTLAND'S RECENT PAST

Edited by

BILLY KAY

POLYGON BOOKS

Polygon Books gratefully acknowledge the assistance of B.B.C. Radio Scotland in the production of this book.

Cover design by
James Hutcheson

Layout
Nigel Billen, Norman Chalmers, Adam Griffin

ISBN 0 904919 55 2

Typeset 11/12 Bembo by
Edinburgh University Student Publications Board

Printed by
H. Charlesworth & Co. Ltd., Huddersfield.

First published in 1982 by
Polygon Books, 1 Buccleuch Place, Edinburgh, EH8 9LW.

The publisher acknowledges subsidy from the Scottish Arts Council towards the publication of this volume.

Contents

Introduction

'Odyssey has attempted to give history back to the people who made it, allowing them to speak without interruption or editing by an "expert" from outside their culture. It has also given them the central role in broadcasting where they have been ignored for so long. As a generation, these people tholed appalling housing, unemployment, decimation by war and abject poverty to survive with their spirit intact. Through their words, programmes full of honesty, vitality and beauty have emerged, helped by the guiding hand of knowledge and commitment shared by all those who have contributed to this book. I have grown to appreciate even more Scotland's interwoven tapestry of cultures, and have learned from the experience I have had collecting the people's stories. If I have succeeded in reflecting truthfully their enduring human dignity in adversity, then Odyssey has been worthy of them.'

The concluding words of my introduction to the first Odyssey book also serves as a declaration of intent for the present volume and the radio series which inspired it. Yet no matter how strong the material which supports the statement may be, it is interpreted as nostalgia by many an academic historian and media elitist. Having filed it under 'nostalgia', the significance of the material is diminished and dismissed as the fanciful ramblings of old men and women. Giving a talk on Odyssey at one of our newer universities I was confronted with a historian of the old school for whom the document is sacred, and who attacked my case for the use of oral sources in history with the zeal of a defender of the faith. His argument could be paraphrased as follows: old folk's memories are subjective and faulty, when interviewed they tell you what you want to hear and exaggerate to please you more — the resulting transcripts are therefore of no historical value. I conceded that memory could be faulty but facts could be verified against other interviewees or indeed against documentary sources. I argued that oral sources were no more or less subjective than the individuals who brought their own bias to bear on the version of events they wrote down; making the resulting documents approved by the historian as the objectively empirical, in fact little more than ideological constructions. Neither documentary nor oral sources should therefore be held sacrosanct, but regarded rather as complementary yet mutually corrective. On the specific question of exaggeration, I asked him to listen to 'The Clydebank Blitz' which was broadcast that week. There, the enormity of the tragedy had been internalised by the people who experienced it, and for them to exaggerate on any aspect of the subject would have been obscene. Instead, with mutual trust, I recorded harrowing images of a muted intensity which one finds only in the

realm of personal experience, and therefore in oral history. When the only history you have is oral, then the desire is to tell it correctly as affectation would belie the importance of the history and demean the people you represent. In subjects such as 'Gallipoli', where few people remain who can tell the story at first hand, the obligation is not only to record those experiences accurately, but quickly, so that this 'living' version of the event is preserved. For so many incidents crucial to the lives of the masses, there remains no historical record of their participation, except in terms of statistics. That is why the extension of oral history despite its imperfections is essential now, if a democratic perspective on our recent past is to be achieved. Pressure of time on the production of the original radio programmes means that one must be selective in the number of people interviewed, limiting in the time spent with them and aware of contradictory and distorted versions of a story. Yet with careful sifting it is possible to distil the essence of an historical moment from a few people, because the importance the moment held for them will be expressed with honesty and passion. The programmes cannot tell every side of the story, but they do offer starting points on many subjects which would remain underground if Odyssey did not exist.

Within the terms of the Academy, we have here examples of oral tradition, labour, military, craft, minority, industrial and migrant history. But what makes all these subjects come dramatically alive is the extent to which they are personalised through the sharing of a subjective experience. Henri Thierry regarded the people as 'both the victims of history and its ultimate arbiters'. The individual reminiscences collected for Odyssey take on a greater symbolic significance, in that they become a statement for the whole group who experienced an historical incident. Thus the survivors of Gallipoli are the 'arbiters and judges' of those who made their fellows victims of that disastrous campaign. Thus Federico Pontiero's description of what it felt like to be arrested as an alien while his baby is dying, becomes a plea for social justice for all minorities and an end to brutal discrimination. Thus the sense of loss of community and loss of work expressed by the people of Clydebank or Glengarnock becomes a lament for a sense of belonging which the modern urban planners and economists cannot build into a place, a belonging which appears to supply a need deep rooted in the human character.

In Clan Neil of Barra, we witness how one person can express a sense of belonging to a community in a centuries-old tradition. In Nan McKinnon's narrative subjective 'truth' and the collective 'imagination' of her culture merge, yet she relates events which preceded even her great-grandmother's birth by hundreds of years, with a precise surety which reveal the knowledge or *mutho logos* of a predominantly oral culture. The fact that a historian can pinpoint her vivid recreation of the McNeil raids on Shetland to within a decade of the fifteenth century from documentary sources indicates not only the accuracy of oral transmission over such a large space of time, but also the need for all historians to admit to the validity of oral sources. The document gives a factual account, Nan McKinnon paints a word picture which makes the event dramatically alive.

With subjects which deal with rural society, there could be a danger of allowing the beauty of place and subject in e.g. 'The Pearl Fishers' to colour how we examine the relationships within that craft. But while Betsy Whyte's lore of pearling is delightful, it is balanced with her memory of the travellers' running conflict with the figures of authority on the river banks. Yet for the dogmatic Marxist who sees history only in terms of class struggle, there is the salutory and perhaps chastening lesson in that chapter that the travelling folk felt a greater affinity with the landed aristocracy than with those closer to their own social order. Perhaps this is a remnant or folk memory of the older paternalist clan system, in which the travellers played such an important role. Similarly, Annie Finlayson's idyllic picture of the herring lassies sitting knitting on a hillside in the long Shetland gloaming is countered with Eveline Crockett's memory of the long-term effects of young girls lifting heavy barrels. There can be no escapism or romantic yearning for a rose-tinted vision of the past because for the majority of Jock Tamson's Bairns there was more struggle than stability in that past. The trap of romanticising the past is easier avoided by those of the same background as the informants, whose recognition of a directness of utterance dictates the same kind of honesty in those collating the material.

Odyssey attempts to portray a multi-dimensional reality, a democratic range of experience, un-conditioned by what I consider to be false divisions. I recall a conversation I had with one respected broadcaster who felt that all the natural poetry in the Odyssey tapes came from those who dwelt in a rural setting, people with a linguistic range and fluency untenable by the urban working class. His is an erroneous belief rooted in middle-class philosophy since the dawn of the Romantic movement — that the peasantry is pure and unspoiled, the harbingers of our traditional culture in a form untainted by either intellectual sophistication or industrial debasement. Herder, the great eighteenth-century German folklorist, summed up the prejudice succinctly in this description of the urban masses: 'The mob in the streets, which never sings or composes but shrieks and mutilates, is not the people.' James Myatt's story of the mongol boy barefoot in the snow in 'Whisky's Awa'?' is told with an eloquent humanity which belies the notion of the urban working class as inarticulate, while the sentiment expressed reveals humanity overcoming conditions that

could crush it. The people are the people, town and country.

For socialists it would be easy to idealise the struggle of the urban workers to gain social justice against the power of impersonal coal companies as in 'Mungo Mackay and the Green Table' or against the State as in 'The '26'. But in Mackay's Midlothian we reveal a working class split down the middle in its attitude to a figure of autocratic authority. There are those who find stability in 'knowing their place', their attitudes to the manager mingled with respect and fear. There are those who regarded his reign as tyrannical, a heinous crime against individual liberty. Both sides are the people. The East Fife miners' communities in 'The '26' stress their solidarity and organised physical resistance to the State, clearly defining themselves to separate themselves from the known groups of blacklegs who capitulated. In the making of that programme stories of the '26 were often mingled with those of the 1922 lock-out. Such memory lapses could be used as ammunition against oral history, but it does reveal an important psychological attitude of the miners towards the period; that both events are linked as one era of unrelenting struggle. A recent project on the 1972 miners' victory against the Government showed that the old miners saw it as revenge for the defeats of '22 and '26, revealing the inter relatedness of all historical events shared by a homogeneous group of people.

In a truly democratic history, there can also be no limiting of 'the people' to specific ethnic groups. As Mr Stone in 'Glasgow Jewry' puts it, "Och, the sufferings of the poor Jews wasn't any more than the sufferings of the Glasgow underfed population." Having suffered early on in their history from that very Scottish institution, the Presbyterian Sabbath, both the Jews and Italians have contributed, and still contribute, to the welcome diversity which is Scotland, in their own unique ways. They too are the people. But where, you may ask, are the rest of the people — the landowners, statesmen, officers, socialites, aristocrats and all the other myriad manifestations of humanity? The answer lies in the thousands of books which surround you. They already have their history, written for and by themselves.

We are concerned with building a history from below. With the material supplied in these Odyssey chapters we are gradually collecting the means by which we can understand our society from within. We are not yet at the stage where we can draw all the conclusions about what the recent past has to offer the present. In collecting this evidence, however, we shall be able to provide those with a commitment to the Scottish tradition with the raw material of human experience to help them understand our past. Each subject to emerge from the Odyssey series will eventually reveal the vivid mosaic which is Scottish life this century. Oral history has been called the spectre which haunts the corridors of the Academy; from the evidence in this book, the spectre is now flesh, bone, and blood.

BILLY KAY

The Clydebank Blitz

On the clear moonlit nights of March 13th and 14th, 1941, over 200 Heinkel 111 and Junker 88 bombers, led by the crack pathfinder unit Kampf Gruppe 100, left bases in France, Holland, North Germany, Denmark and Norway; their destination Clydebank. Clydebank was the first Scottish town to experience the full horror of total war, and forty years on, the physical and mental scars on the place and the people still endure.

Clydebank Town Council had initially been slow to respond to the threat of war. From 1935 to 1937, while other local authorities prepared for civil defence, the Town Council, with the support of the local Labour M.P. David Kirkwood, adhered to the Socialist view that compliance with the right wing National Government Directive was tantamount to condoning its foreign policy and recognising the inevitability of war. The same pacifist stance had been part of the philosophy of the so-called 'Red Clydesiders' during the First World War, and Kirkwood, one of the activists during that period, emphasised his determination to avoid immersing his constituents in the carnage of war. During a pre-election speech in October 1935 he asserted, 'I am all out for peace in the real sense and would not send a Clydebank boy to war upon any consideration. No war for me under any circumstances.' This view was reiterated by Kirkwood's Party leader George Lansbury when he addressed the Labour Party Conference that same month: 'Those who take to the sword shall perish by the sword.'

By January 1937 Clydebank was one of only three recalcitrant local authorities left in Scotland, and it was not until the Government assumed compulsory powers later in the year that the town, potentially one of the prime industrial targets in the U.K., finally carried out Civil Defence preparations.

James Hastings was Depute Town Clerk at the time:
"Once the 1937 Act came into being, we certainly got the go-ahead from the Town Council and we got any support that we needed from them; they not only supported us, they pushed us almost to exhaustion. The net result was that they were in the forefront of the local authorities with their preparations by the time 1939 and 1940 came along."

By the time of the Blitz there were 462 A.R.P. (Air Raid Precaution) wardens in the burgh, of whom fifty were employed on a full-time basis. These wardens co-ordinated the various services which were formed — ambulance teams, rescue squads, decontamination squads, Auxiliary Fire Service, First Aid Posts and A.R.P. Wardens Posts. Houses with gardens were provided with Anderson shelters, huts of various sizes made of curved corrugated steel sheets which were sunk into the ground. The majority of the town's residents, however, were crowded into one- and two-roomed houses in tenements, and these people in the main relied on the ground-floor closes of the buildings for shelter. These entries were reinforced with steel and guarded at either side with baffle walls which prevented splinter from blast entering the closes. Concrete surface shelters were also built, but most folk preferred the cosiness and companionship of the closes. The Clydebank tenements, despite the overcrowding, had developed an intimate communal culture of mutual self-help, something which the Bankies still recall with warmth.

Mrs Richardson:
"Clydebank was a great place, really was. In Clydebank you never walked anywhere but you always got, 'Hello'—always did. Didn't matter what you were, up high or down low, you were always classed the same. Up each tenement close there was nine families—a bedroom and a kitchen, that was all. The toilet was outside on the stair, that's the way everybody lived at that time."

Miss Docherty:
"There was a lot to be said for the old tenement buildings. People cared about each other. John Knox Street was always full of characters, good, down to earth, solid folk."

The 'clarty but cosy' familiarity and bustling energy of the town with its self-contained communities such as 'The Holy City' was like a magnet to people brought

Kilbowie Road, c. 1937.

German bomber over the North Sea.

up there, so much so that several families evacuated to the safety of the country at the beginning of the war, returned to Clydebank despite the imminent danger of aerial attack.

Patrick Donnelly:

"At the beginning o' the war, the whole family were evacuated to Tighnabruach, that's across from Rothesay, and we stayed there for a few month. We couldn't stick the country life kinda thing, we stayed in the Marquis o' Bute's house; it was like a big haunted house and we couldn't really stand it. I think most people actually came home. You've got your home and it doesn't really matter how bad things are, you'll just go back to it and just accept it."

During the first year of the 'phoney war' the returnees' decision was vindicated, and people got used to sirens sounding for false alarms or nothing more than the odd German reconnaissance plane. Shortly before the March raids, however, many noticed increased activity above Clydebank.

Father Sheary:

"A couple of weeks before the Blitz took place, something like lights came down as if German planes were taking photographs of Singers and the Clydebank area in general. We were all out watching the way the sky was all lighted up and we were actually saying to ourselves, they must be preparing to come to blitz us."

Mr Bain:

"There was an apprentices' strike on in the Clyde shipyards and the weather couldn't have been better, it was like a summer's day in March and we played a lot of football in the afternoon. Well, I was in the Royal Artillery at the time, on ack-ack, so we were trained for spottin' planes. On the Tuesday afternoon I think it was, there was a plane flying pretty high, and I said, well, it looked like a JU 88—it definitely to me was a reconnaissance plane going over but never thought any more about it. But I've thought plenty of it since, because of what happened on the Thursday night."

The day and evening of the raid were like any other. Many Bankies were at the pictures and dancing when the raid began, presuming the sirens signalled yet another false alarm. For those outside, it was clearly visible that this night would be different.

Mrs Bain:

"When the raid started my sister and I were over in Blanefield and that's on the other side o' the Old Kilpatrick Hills from here. And we were with two boyfriends and one o' them drove a car. It was the sky, the sky was all lit wi' red, just a red glow in the sky, and comin' over Windy Hill, you could see the whole o' the Clyde Valley. Clydebank seemed to be all on fire."

Miss Docherty:

"The siren went about nine o'clock in the evening and at home my mother was in, my two sisters and myself and we thought, it was just another raid, you know, the sirens had gone before and nothing had ever happened. But before many minutes had passed, things began to fall down from the wall, glass splintering and my mother decided that we'd better really go downstairs into the close."

Despite anti-aircraft fire which kept the planes at a height which normally would have prevented accurate bombing, the perfect visibility and perhaps a measure of luck, resulted in incendiaries setting alight the Yoker distillery at one end of the town, the Admiralty oil storage tanks at the other end, with Singer's wood yard providing the third beacon in the town centre. The bombers ran up and down the line of the blazes, dropping 272 tons of high explosives and 1,650 incendiary containers, the latter described by an eye witness as falling 'like raindrops in a storm or locusts settling upon ripe grain'. To the people in the tenements below it was the beginning of a night of hell.

Miss Docherty:

"Oh dear, the noise was dreadful. I don't remember much until about midnight, it was well past bedtime of course and my mother put me down in a corner to sleep and she said that she was going out to the close for a breath of air and that was the last time I saw her. When I woke up I thought I was still in my bed and tried to, to turn over, but here the clothes seemed very very tight somehow, you know how you pull? My hands were full of stones and they were hot at that. Oh, I knew there was something not right here and I shouted for my mother. Of course there was no answer. Then away down below me I heard my sister calling me and she told me that we had been hit by a landmine and that we were buried away and the building was on fire and she told me to shout as loudly as I could. I seemed to be sinking into unconsciousness, you know, off and on, but my sister made me come awake and we called out and called for help and I couldn't get my leg free, it was caught in one of those big girders and I was told later that every rope they put down burnt in front of their eyes. So I was going into unconsciousness until I heard Father White—one of the curates in the church at the time—and two men speaking, saying, 'Father, we'll break her legs if we pull her like this!' And he said—I remember his answer well—'If she's to come out without her legs she'll have to come because the two of them will burn!' Well, when I heard that I'm telling you I fought like a tigress trying to free myself. Then I remember them pulling, pulling, pulling and with a final tug I came out. And it was an easy matter then for them to go down and pick out my sister because I had been

lying on top of her. So we were taken then to the Rest Centre in Elgin Street and that I'll never forget. The noise and the screams and the cries and in particular I remember my godmother who owned a wee sweetie shop at the corner of Napier Street, and the last I saw of her, her arm was severed from there—and the screams of her . . . and even as a child, I'll, I'll always remember the silence when she died."

Bridget McHard:

"Well I just remember this chap that stayed in the close, John Green was his name, tellin' us to cover wir heads—he saw something through the shutters of the window. Well, I remember putting my hands over my head and puttin' my head down, and that's all I remember until I wakened up and I was buried. It was a funny experience really, I was buried in my mouth and nose, my face down, but I remember wakening up and this terrible dust—in fact I don't like dust from that time. I don't like dust. I seemed to come and go an awful lot. But I know I wasn't taken out until three o'clock on Friday afternoon, and that was from midnight the night before. The only time I saw daylight was when I was gettin' pulled out and I could feel the thing comin' over ma face when I was gettin' pulled out. I'd one brother on one side of me and a sister on the other side of me—they were both killed. But my mother was buried, she was in a cavity sittin' on a chair. The buildin' was on fire and wi' the firemen playin' the hose on the fire and the way my mother was situated, it was like a cavity, and it just filled up with water. My young sister was on her knee and she said that when she felt herself goin' away, or fainting, her hands slipped. She was tryin' to hold onto my sister Eveline and when she was dug out she was sorta pulled up the way and as she looked down she saw Eveline lyin' where she'd fell off her knee and she just told the man that that was her wee girl. So if

'Clydebank seemed to be all on fire.'

What was Tennant's pub. Corner of Radnor Street and Robertson Street.

she wasn't killed then she was drowned because the water had come right up to my mother's mouth, she'd tae hold her head up. So that obviously Eveline, if she wasn't killed, she was drowned."

Father Sheary:

"One of the tragic stories is about a family called Semple, and Mrs Semple had quite a large family and they were all young. On that night, she had one in either arm and one on either side of her and she was standing in a close and I think it was an aerial torpedo that struck against Jericho Street, but the blast that came from that took a child out of her right arm and took the child at her left side, leaving her with the child in her left arm and a child on her right side. They two escaped, she escaped and she never saw as much as a rip of hair belonging to the other two children. Frightening; I'll never forget that as long as I live. They disappeared completely —she never saw them again, never, not so much as a rip of hair belonging to them, poor woman."

Mrs Hyslop:

"A couple came to me—their wee boy . . . they had got out, but he hadn't got out and they came to me, I think it must have been the day after. He was in Graham Avenue, so I said, 'Well, you go back and I'll get the lads to have a look'—they told me where to look. And he had been playing wi' marbles and that's what identified him was his marbles. He had been burned. And it was just bones really that were left. So, they were a Catholic family, terribly worried about him, so we got the wee remains put in a wee box got them buried as they would have liked and when they came back I said 'Yes'—we'd found him. I didn't say how we had found him, and I said, 'Everything was done that you would have done.' There was that wee boy just sittin' playin' wi' his marbles, and that had to happen to him."

The tenement homes became death traps with whole families wiped out in one explosion. The shelters undoubtedly saved many lives during the first night of the Blitz, but only providence could save those near the place of impact of a landmine or bomb. For many, in the microcosm of the Anderson shelters, however, it was possible to remain innocently ignorant of what was going on outside.

Willie Green:

"That first night in the shelter in the Rolls Royce [factory] it was quite remarkable because we found out there was quite a number of talented people, girls, who were singing opera stuff, of that quality —it was unbelievable. And of course whenever a bomb went off there was hysterics, you know, the girls screaming and the men saying 'Everything's alright', and then probably encourage the girls to sing again. We had no sort of inclination what was happening upstairs."

Kilbowie Road, looking north.

Mrs Richardson:

"We used to sit in the shelters and play guessin' games and sing and then 'I Spy'—used to laugh—'I Spy' in the dark! We'd light candles and once we got the 'I Spy', the candle would be put out again and then lit again. And then the sing-songs, it was all the old-fashioned songs, used to love to hear the old folks singing—you know. My mother used to sing 'The Old Rowan Tree', that was her song."

Mary Rodgers:

"There was a church soiree and some of the audience went out and they thought they would be safer in the shelter. And others stayed in the church hall. When the all-clear went, the people were just sittin' like mummies. The door had got blasted off and the blast went in and the people were just sittin' like mummies in their seats there."

Willie Green:

"During a lull in the early morning I went up above ground and I saw Clydebank burnin'—complete panic. People don't talk much about their fears but I can assure you I was scared that night, and more so I think being helpless. You know, if you had a crossbow and just firin' aimlessly, you'd feel you're sorta doing something, but just to sit there. . . ."

The feeling of impotence expressed by Mr Green was shared by a majority of the citizens, who saw little sign of defensive measures being taken, dismissing the guns at Auchentoshan and Dentiglennan as brave but hopelessly inadequate, but praising the 'tram' system of decoys which diverted many bombs to the Old Kilpatrick Hills. The main resistance seems to have come from a Polish destroyer which happened to be in the basin for repair that first night. Clydebank was the first major raid on a Scottish town. It acted as an unfortunate guinea pig, the authorities discovering faults in the system which were only remedied for future attacks.

James Hastings:

"We had, let's say, about 300 or 400 [incidents] —and we only had about ten rescue teams, perhaps

Rowan Tree

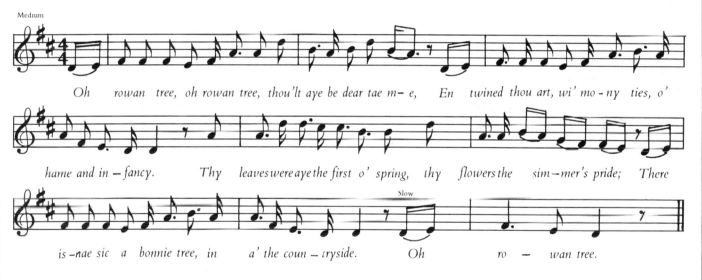

Oh rowan tree, oh rowan tree, thou'lt aye be dear tae m-e, En twined thou art, wi' mo-ny ties, o' hame and in-fancy. Thy leaves were aye the first o' spring, thy flowers the sim-mer's pride; There is-nae sic a bonnie tree, in a' the coun-tryside. Oh ro-wan tree.

How fair wert thou in simmer time, wi' all thy clusters white,
How rich and gay thy autumn dress, wi' berries red and bright.
On thy fair stem were mony names which now nae mair I see,
But there engraven on my heart, forgot they ne'er can be.

We sat aneath the spreading shade, the bairnies round thee ran,
They pu'd thy bonnie berries red and necklaces they strang.
My mither oh I see her still, she smiled our sports to see,
Wi' little Jeanie on her lap, and Jamie at her knee.

Oh there arose my faither's pray'r in holy evening's calm,
How sweet was then my mither's voice in the martyr's psalm.
Now a' are gane! We meet nae mair aneath the rowan tree,
But hallowed thoughts around thee twine, o' hame and infancy.

ten fire appliances, half a dozen or more ambulances—first aid parties, perhaps another ten or so—that we just couldn't cope, and why I say that the thing was chaotic outside was that they had all been sent out and there was nothing more we could do until reinforcements came in from outside. The telephones went—we were dependent on runners. And these were just young lads, they weren't supposed to operate while a raid was in progress; in any event, instead of perhaps twenty or thirty of them reporting, there was only a few reported because, quite naturally, when their houses had been bombed and there was a chance of more aircraft coming over—their parents weren't going to let them out of the shelters to go through a raid to come down and work with us. So communication was just absolutely hopeless. There were fires all over the place, you see, hot ashes from domestic fires got in among the debris from a building, this set it alight. Sometimes the explosion itself had fractured a gas main and set the gas mains alight. My impression was that the whole town was on fire and very little was being done about it. But it transpired that what had happened was the fire engines had run out of petrol—there were only two pumps left in the whole town that weren't damaged. They couldn't get petrol, they'd been hauling the hoses, the wet hoses over debris that included a lot of glass and nails and sharp edges, a lot of their hoses were torn to bits. We found another thing and that was that a lot of the equipment that came in from other areas to help us out, their appliances couldn't be coupled up to our mains because there was no standardisation of mains

outlets and fire hydrants in Scotland. So quite a lot of them were standing about doing absolutely nothing. They just could not operate."

Mrs Hyslop:
"Unfortunately the First Aid Post got a hit, so of course the folks all knew me—'Right, we'll go to the Warden's Post'. And about two or three o'clock in the morning, a young woman walked in, she came over to me because I had a white helmet, wanted to know—where was the doctor. So I explained to her this was a warden's post, not a First Aid Post and there was no doctor—and she walked away. I'm sorry to this day that I didn't find out who that young woman was because she went, as I learned later, to the hospital and said 'Look, boys, Clydebank's needing you', and between five and six in the morning, I realised here was men coming in putting on white jackets. They were medical students sitting their exams—and she must have had a job getting her way from our place to the Western Infirmary because there was craters that she would have to dodge with her wee car. I didn't have much time to go out on the streets but I went out periodically just to check how things were. That was Second Avenue there got a direct hit and the place was just obliterated."

Father Sheary:
"The second night of the Blitz was terrifying; as darkness fell, the whole of Singers from Kilbowie Road right up to the boundary of St Stephen's, it was all wood, and it had been hit with the incendiaries the day before. During the daylight we

Above: A blitzed family with their belongings. Opposite: Dalmuir West tramway terminus.

Evacuees queueing for buses in Glasgow Road.

didn't notice the fire but as darkness came over it, it appeared more like the inferno itself. The red blaze of the burning wood and the darkness of the night."

Willie Green:

"It is a traumatic experience, you know, because you see the town you've lived with disappearing. In Scotland I think this is the only place, except Greenock and Paisley—a whole community you knew and grew up in, things that you'd known all your life, suddenly disappeared."

Mrs Richardson:

"Right from Second Avenue right up to about Radnor Street, all these houses were down, and it really was full of people lying about. Sometimes you seen just trouser legs or legs or arms—and as you went up Kilbowie Road, you know, the bombs had fell there and it was wee tram cars used to run up round there and the tram lines were up, you know, like a jigsaw. And then, right along Crown Avenue, I think there were about three closes left in Crown Avenue standing, the same down Second Avenue, just two closes left. And you think back— 'Did you come through that or did you not?'."

Over 1,200 people lost their lives on Clydeside on these nights, 534 of them belonging to Clydebank itself. Fortunately, thousands of Bankies were evacuated before the second night's raid, which was even more intensive. Of the burgh's 12,000 houses, only eight remained completely untouched by the bombing. Several people remember standing on the hills surrounding Clydebank, at Gleniffer and Old Kilpatrick, watching their community being devastated. Whether achieved by the authorities or by the people themselves 'trekking' away, the evacuation was efficient and immediately effective, as the population dropped from 50,000 to 2,000 in two days. With unexploded bombs lying around and the threat of another raid ever present, it was a relief for the people to get out of the area.

Mr Bain:

"Clydebank on the following day after the first night of the Blitz, it was like a nightmare. There was buildings still burning, there was masonry, huge sandstone slabs, you know, had fallen down after the fire. The whole place was really in a turmoil. It's just the look on the people's faces, the lost look, you know, really lost."

Mrs Richardson:

"We were leaving on buses, we didn't know what destination we were going to, we just got on the buses and we were going along Great Western Road and I think the Germans thought it was the Clyde—they mistook the Boulevard for the Clyde, and they were droppin' the bombs and the buses were rockin' back and forward but the bus drivers still kept goin' till we got down and it was Bonhill we'd landed in. Well when we landed in the church they supplied us with beds and blankets, beautiful blankets, and we were all lying around the whole church hall, up the centre. The older people, they put all the young ones down, sorted them in their beds, slept there all night, got up in the morning—we were taken down to the barracks, down at Bonhill, and given breakfasts and those that had to go to work were put on buses and that. We travelled like that all the time, up and down, and they couldn't do enough for us."

Willie Green:
"Anyone who stayed unless they were necessary, was really a handicap. And one of the tragedies, you know, there was a certain amount of looting. Yes, I've heard of people who got stuff stolen. Men were re-fixing the houses, you know, wee simple things were stolen, like the wee tumblers out o' Woolworth's, the wee tumbler stands, the wee things that cost sixpence, things like that were all gettin' removed. It's surprisin', people'll take things."

Mary Rodgers:
"There were people that were saying that they had this in their house and the next thing and it got blitzed. They done away with rubbish and they got new stuff. And they'd lost a fur coat in the Blitz and never had a fur coat in their life! It made you laugh at the time."

If human weakness was displayed in the petty looting that went on, it was the overwhelming memory of human dignity and courage that remained in the minds of most folk.

Mary Rodgers:
"After the raid, there was always people passing our house because we lived on the main Kilbowie Road and people were going away out to the hills. This particular day there was this group and this man obviously had a wooden leg, and he had another leg, a spare leg, and he'd a walking stick. He stood and he took the other leg from under his arm and waved it to us and we thought, well, that man had the courage to wave a wooden leg to us and maybe in his simple way of waving to us it would give us courage. You cried and you laughed at the same time. Then another day we seen this group and they passed the window and there's this man carryin' a good-sized picture of the Pope. And although we were Protestants, my mother started crying. She said to me in Gaelic: his faith is so strong in that picture itself that that man feels that he'll be safe."

Alex Nicolson was one of a group of volunteers from the Edinburgh Council of Social Services who came to lend a hand at an emergency station set up after the blitz at the Town Hall.

Queue at mobile canteen, the morning after.

9

Alex Nicolson:

"Different people were allocated different jobs. And they asked me if I would walk up and down the queue, which was increasing ever moment, trying to find out what the people wanted, because in the hall there were tables with assistants sitting taking information, and I could direct them to the [correct] table. If they wanted immediate financial help because all their money had gone, if they wanted to go to stay with relatives, if they needed clothing, food, or information about their own relatives, or to give information of people whom they knew had been killed. If we could get any direct information and just hand it over it saved the people waiting in the queue. I've never seen such dignity, such courage and I didn't hear a grumble that whole day. During all this walking up and down, feeling perfectly useless but at least presumably doing something—I'd been into the hall with information and was standing in the door just coming out again when a man came up to me and gave me a bit of paper and said— 'This is the name of a child who was picked up in a shelter—dead. Would you take it in?' And I said, 'You're quite sure that this is right and the child was dead?', and he said, 'Yes. She was picked up beside my own bairn who was dead too.' And then he stood for a moment and said, 'We're not going to do this to German people's bairns, are we? What good is that going to do?' And I thought, the *courage* of it. There was no resentment, there was no bitterness, it was just a thought, about other people's children."

Undefeated.

The morale of the people remained high, aided by the fact that their jobs were secure. Even those evacuated to thirty miles beyond, managed to turn up for the morning shift when industry resumed a few days later. Bombs hit the Royal Ordnance Factory at Dalmuir, the asbestos works and several other targets, but the raid failed to hinder war production to any great extent. Yet for the people who returned to the town there was no escaping the omnipresent images of tragedy. At Dalnottar Cemetery a communal grave was established, where many unidentifiable bodies were buried, with priests and ministers in attendance for days afterwards. People wandered once familiar streets, looking for traces of a life irrevocably lost.

Father Sheary:

"I had married one of the Dorans just shortly before the Blitz and I was talking to him on the morning of the 14th and he went up to try and find his parents and they were blown to atoms. Two or three weeks afterwards I met him, I went back to see what was left of Dalmuir and I didn't know the place, to be honest with you—couldn't find out which was First Terrace, Second Terrace, or Third Terrace. But I saw Denis Doran and he was with his two hands pulling away there, bricks and mortar—and I said, 'What are you doing?' 'I'm looking,' he said, 'for a rip of hair belonging to my family'."

For those remaining alive, a long wait ensued before the authorities found the resources to rebuild the devastated town. A natural resentment developed among those who could compare the aftermath of the Clydebank Blitz with that of other cities which had suffered a similar fate during the war.

Mrs Hyslop:

"Clydebank never got a chance to rebuild. And where Coventry and lots of towns in England which were badly bombed, were given the money to rebuild, Clydebank wasn't."

Miss Docherty:

"Later on in years I went to Italy via Germany and we stopped off at Essen. Really and truly I nearly lost my eyesight. It was built beautifully! The shops were full of goods, and everyone seemed to be so well off, and that stayed in my mind because when I came back to Clydebank after my holiday, there we were, b'God, still sitting in the rubble."

The town was eventually rebuilt, but the communal culture of the tenements with its closely knit family groups could never return. Instead, people were scattered into ill-planned housing schemes where the impersonality of the environment produced in many a sense of isolation. The same could be said of many towns. In Clydebank, however, the possibly nostalgic memory the people have of the pre-war community is

Funeral of unknown victims at the communal grave, Dalnottar Cemetery.

overwrought with the terrible personal tragedies most families were touched by. It is a tragedy I felt in Clydebank. Because of the intimate personal nature of the people's reminiscences, I became more emotionally involved with this programme than any other before or since, aware of the tension between telling the true horror of the story while remaining sensitive to the trust the people placed in me. Today, the Blitz is still a potent memory for the Clydebank people, one which will die only when those who lived through it die themselves.

Father Sheary:

"It took me three years to get over the nervous reaction that set in as a result of that. Every time I'd hear a plane, even in peace time, when it came I used to go to pieces for long enough because of the effect that the bombers and the bombs had upon me on that occasion, the 13th and 14th of March."

Bridget McHard:

"I had three sisters, three brothers, there was five of them killed in the Blitz, and my father was killed in the Blitz as well. It was really only my mother and I that survived out the building. My mother and I became very close through it. She still gets upset every March, you know, gets depressed—she's eighty-one now."

Patrick Donnelly:

"I was twelve at the time. Always remember carrying my young sister up to school, Margaret, that was my favourite. We were a pretty close family, you know, up to the Blitz, and that was it. It was terrible. I would say that, for the next three years that I could see myself walking down the streets o' Helensburgh, on my own, and I'd burst out cryin'—it really took me years to get over it. To think I actually had four sisters and a brother, my mother, and that was me completely on my own."

Miss Docherty:

"When I think of the 13th of March, 1941, I often say to myself—that one night changed our whole life. The family, you would say, never ever got together again as a family should be, and when we did we were all changed. I would love to have known my sister and my brother and my mother as a grown-up. In my family, my mother was killed, she was thirty-nine; my eldest sister, she was killed—she was about twenty-two, and my eldest brother was killed, he was just coming up for twenty-one. And I always thought of the old song—'The Flowers o' the Forest are a' Weed Awa'."

BILLY KAY

Italiani in Scozzia

Italians have a long and varied history in Scotland. They first came to prominence in the wake of the Renaissance in the sixteenth century and it has been established that James IV and VI, both much influenced by Italian culture, employed Italian minstrels to entertain the *literati* who attended the court at Holyroodhouse. Royal favour of a different kind was bestowed upon the ill-fated David Rizzio, ex-Piedmontese musician and counsel to Mary, Queen of Scots. But it was in the eighteenth century, during the so-called 'revolution of manners', that Italian culture achieved its strongest hold. A contemporary writer claimed that 'every girl in Edinburgh who plays the pianoforte learns Italian, and Italian masters are to be found in every street'. The greatest of these was the renowned Italian tenor, Giusto Ferdinando Tenducci, who settled in Edinburgh in 1770. For champions of the native muse, such as the poet Fergusson, the popularity of Italian culture was regarded as a threat. Fergusson satirised the dandies who followed Italian fashion as 'macaronies' and launched a bitter attack on the impact of Italian music in his 'Elegy on the Death of Scots Music':

> Now foreign sonnets bear the gree,
> And crabbed queer variety
> Of sounds fresh sprung frae Italy,
> A bastard breed!
> Unlike that saft-tongu'd melody
> Which now lies dead.

But this influence had been nurtured by a tiny musical élite over the years and it was not until the nineteenth century that the number of Italians increased. The contrast with their well-respected and illustrious predecessors could hardly have been greater. As itinerant street-musicians and entertainers, pedlars of plaster statuettes, organ-grinders and chestnut-sellers, the Italian migrants, dependent as much on their wits as on their trade to earn a living, travelled from town to town on a circuit that covered most of Britain. The sojourn in Scotland was brief and it was only towards the end of the century that Italian migration took on a more permanent form. Thereafter, growth was rapid and between 1890 and 1914 the Italian population in Scotland increased from 750 to over 4,500.

The vast majority of the immigrants to arrive in Scotland after 1880 were peasants from two quite distinct areas of Italy, some 250 miles apart: the province of Lucca in northern Italy and Frosinone in the Abruzzi, south of Rome. The tradition of seasonal or temporary migration was common in these areas but the decision to move further afield, to emigrate overseas, was prompted by the rapid growth in population in the last quarter of the century and the consequent increase in the level of economic hardship. For some, life there was no longer acceptable.

Federico Pontiero:

"My father, he had eight of a family. He was a peasant and of course somebody had to go oot, you

Opposite: The Hokey Pokey man. 'When they sold this ice-cream, they would say, 'Ecce un poco, Senore'. And the people would interpret that as Hokey Pokey'.—Dominic Crolla. Above: Corn harvest in Picinisco.

Ice-cream parlour, Edinburgh, c. 1925.

know, of the family. So he says, 'You canna make a living here the way I make a living on this small amount of land that I've got. So some of you has got to go somewhere else to make a start in life.' I was glad to come here [Cambuslang], I mean to make some kinda progress in life for my ambition was to live the proper way, no' the rough way. . . ."

Mrs D'Agostino:
"I have only flashes of childhood in Italy. I remember the vast countryside, full of grape-vines, lots of trees and animals and chickens. I used to run wild. I remember running barefooted but there was no such thing as hunger because they grew so much. There was poverty though, it was a terrible struggle. I mean if someone took ill or if someone needed an operation, you had to sell a cow or sell one of your mules and that was a great hardship because they would need it. Everyone was more or less the same, glad to escape the hard life they had over in Italy."

The most common route to Scotland at the turn of the century was via London, which was the main centre of Italian settlement in Britain at that time.

Dominic Crolla:
"I had a friend in Edinburgh whose father, when he died, we were all up in his house at night and we were looking for his birth certificate. When we came across it in a drawer we discovered that his father in 1904 or 1905 had been born on the roadside between Dover and London. You see these people had walked from Italy, they'd got lifts on horses and carts and they made their way from the middle of Italy by road and track and boat to London."

Other immigrants came by a more direct route under a system of contract labour organised by recruiting agents in Italy who were in the pay of the *padroni* (employers or patrons) based in London. It seems likely that it was through the *padroni* system that the Italians first came to be associated with the ice-cream trade in Scotland.

Alfonso Barsotti:
"I can remember my dad telling me that a couple of men came into the village an' they were talkin' away, 'We've got these places if you're interested, we can give ye work'. And they started describing the places, that there were theatres and big shops

Ice-cream parlour, Glasgow, c. 1925.

ice-cream and its Italian associations with considerable misgivings.

The most vociferous complaints came from the United Free Church who condemned the Italians for keeping their shops open on Sundays thereby challenging what was regarded as sacrosanct, namely, Sabbath observance. Furthermore, it was alleged that moral as well as spiritual values were under threat. In evidence to a Parliamentary Committee on Sunday Trading in 1906, it was suggested that ice-cream parlours might be 'morally contaminating' as 'young people of both sexes congregate there after legitimate hours and sometimes misbehave themselves . . . that is the one great attraction of the ice-cream shops and not the ingredient itself'. The police also added their weight to the opposition. Standards of behaviour in ice-cream shops, it was claimed, were low and were 'acceptable only to their alien owners and to people of loose moral habits'.

The ice-cream traders responded by joining forces with the Temperance movement. Although Temperance slogans such as 'lips that touch liquor shall never touch mine' had never had much of an appeal among the majority of the working class, Temperance reformers still continued to encourage alternatives to the temptations of the public house. In 1907 the 'Temperance Refreshment Traders Defence Association' was set up and an appeal, which contained the signatures of over 800 Italian traders in Scotland, was lodged against any change in the legislation. But the pious rhetoric of the sabbatarians were a mere adjunct to a carefully orchestrated and lengthy campaign conducted by the Shop Assistants' Union — a campaign which culminated in the Shops Act 1911 and Sunday closure.

In comparison with the hostility which jaundiced the experience of the Irish and the Lithuanians on their arrival in Scotland the Italians were well received. Anti-alien prejudice appears to have been suspended primarily because the Italians, in the occupations they followed, never represented a serious threat to native labour or wages. Nonetheless minor incidents did take place.

Mrs McGillivray:
"When I used to go to school the kids used tae pull my hair, I had jet black hair, and [tell me] to speak Italian. I spoke Italian, I couldn't speak anythin' else, I couldn't even tell them to stop it."

Dominic Crolla:
"Many times when the chap would be going round the streets with the barrow they'd get a couple of youths coming up and making a bit of fun because the man couldn't speak English. They'd go up pretending they were going to buy something and when the Italian chap lifted the lid they'd throw bundles of stones or something into the freezer. These boys were only doing it as a prank, you see, but for the Italian man it was a loss of a lot of money because they'd wasted his goods."

and so, of course, all the kids in the village were thinking that this was going to be marvellous. The work, it didnae seem much, they thought just stand out there and sell the ice-cream things instead o' us workin' and sawin' logs and drainin' ground and ploughin'—this is money for nothin'! . . . My dad he was about fourteen when he came over. What, of course, they didnae know was that they'd be workin' practically all day and also [that] there was a guy employed just to make sure they only took their wee breaks whenever they should and that they carried out the work. Everywhere he went there was somebody there, you know, just to watch."

In spite of the difficulties which confronted them some of the pioneer Italians did extremely well. Leopold Guliani from the village of Barga (in Lucca province) is said to have owned over sixty cafés in Scotland and was one of a substantial business group beginning to take shape on Clydeside before 1914. By then the 'Ice-cream Parlour' had become a common feature in most towns and villages in Scotland, for the ice-cream cone, like a drink or a flutter, transcended class differences and was enjoyed by rich and poor alike. There were, however, some sections of the local population who looked upon the growth in the trade of

Occasionally the presence of a group of youngsters could be turned to advantage.

Federico Pontiero:

"At the beginning I mean I stood a lot o' abuse, yes, kids especially, because you couldnae speak. Many's the time though you'd get some o' the young boys, they were very good. I gave them 'pokey-hats' and they gave you a hand to shove it [the barrow] up the hill. Some o' the hills you couldnae really shove it yourself because you were trying to shove it up the way and the barrow was pushing down the way. I even pushed the barrow up the Cathkin Braes one morning and you know how much I made? Two pence! Aye, it was heavy, heavy work and it was quite a wee bit hard life tae build up the business. When I did come here the day start seven in the mornin', didna finish till one o'clock, maybe two o'clock in the mornin' and that was for eight solid year. There were one night we went to the pictures, the three o' us and when we went back home, they told us, 'No more pictures!' We hadna a night off nor nothing. I mind o' Mr Rinaldi, I think he was the first Italian settled in Cambuslang, he used to go down the Clyde there and cut the ice. They cut the ice in the Clyde at that time so it must have been an awfu' number of year ago because I never seen a Clyde frozen since! (laughs) It was breakin' ice off for the ice-cream.

Mrs McGillivray and sister. c. 1910.

Aye it was a struggle, you know, it wasna money made easy I assure you."

In many cases this hard-earned cash was used to pay off a debt or loan from a benefactor who had provided the finance to start the business. In 1891 a benefit society, *Società di Mutuo Soccorso*, was set up in Glasgow mainly for this purpose. It was much more likely that newcomers would receive assistance from relatives or friends already established in Scotland.

Antonio D'Arpino:

"When I came here to Glasgow in 1922 I didn't know a word and I just had the address in ma' hands, and I was workin' for five, six months and after that a friend o' mine says, 'I'll buy a shop, I'll let you into my trade', and that's how I started."

Mrs McGillivray:

"My father came to Edinburgh in 1902 and in those days you could get a shop and some stock for about £150. After a while, he used to open the shops and sell them to the Italian fellows, you know, as a going concern. First of all he took them on as payin' servants [employees] and then, if they were worthy, he sold them the shop and they paid him so much a week, you see, towards the shop becoming theirs."

A crucial element in this financial transaction, which greatly minimised the risk involved in providing the capital, was a knowledge of the newcomer's background. The information was not difficult to obtain.

Dominic Crolla:

"When they came over all the people from their own village would come over to join them, they would settle where their own villagers were, their own friends. So there's a big crowd from Barga, they've gathered together in Glasgow and the West. Most of them that came here to Edinburgh were from the villages in the Abruzzi and they made for the Grassmarket because it was the most similar place to an Italian piazza. So the Italian colony at that time was more or less centred around St Mary's Street, the Pleasance and the Grassmarket. Everybody knew everybody else."

On entering into a business deal, therefore, the newcomer became enmeshed in a web of social contacts which had their origin in the villages of Lucca or the Abruzzi rather than in Glasgow or Edinburgh. Indeed, it was these links that kept the Italian community together as organisation on a more formal basis was extremely difficult due to the widespread dispersal of the immigrants nationally and the nature of their work. Italian societies were few in number prior to the early 1920s and it was through the family that the traditions and customs of the homeland were preserved.

Mrs D'Agostino:

"Your parents were very Italian, of course, all their thinking was Italian. Every Friday we used to have a whole congregation in our back shop and all the old ladies used to get together and have a good old gossip—I mean they missed the village life. They were very pleasant and polite to their customers but they didn't really mix with them. . . . They were very old fashioned and the girls were kept under a strict rule because they felt that everyone here was much too free and easy."

Mrs Lucchesi:

"My father wanted us to be as much Italian as we possibly could. In the house it was definitely Italian, the food was Italian, we spoke Italian, we had Italian friends and we were brought up that we had to marry Italians. It wasn't only our family for that was a general thing with the Italians. My family consisted of six girls and a boy and we all married Italians. The social life, especially for the girls was very restricted. We got on very very well with the Scots boys who came into the shop and have chats with us but then they stopped asking us out because they knew we wouldn't go out. You could almost say it was forbidden."

Mrs McGillivray:

"I met my husband during the 1914-18 war, he was an engineer sub-lieutenant. When he first came into the shop I thought he was a Rear-Admiral, if you please, with all that gold on his arm! Anyway, I got married to him. You know, the Italian community made me an outcast because I married a Scotsman and because he was a Presbyterian and here I was, a Roman Catholic. Because I was an outcast I used to take him to the Italian dances and I used to hear all the Italian ladies say, 'We don't blame her for marryin' him—isn't he handsome!' And was I happy at that bit, I just turned round and smiled. After that I never went near them because I wasn't gonna allow them to slight me."

Parental control, particularly over the choice of marriage partner, remained strong through the 1920s and 1930s. It enhanced the *italianità* of their children and ensured that the tight social organisation of the community, centred round the tradition of *campanilismo* or village loyalties, was maintained.

In the inter-war years the number of new arrivals from Italy was reduced to a trickle by the restrictive Aliens Act of 1919, consequently the Italian population stabilised at a figure of around 5,500. It was a community, therefore, of older, well-established immigrants who had on the whole achieved a certain degree of security. There was also prosperity. For example, between 1911 and 1931 the number of Italian restaurant-keepers had increased from 278 to nearly 700 and by the 1930s the Italian street-vendor had become something of a rarity. With stability and prosperity also came organisational growth.

A wedding procession in Picinisco.

Professional associations such as the *Associazione dei Gelatieri* (Association of Ice-Cream Traders) had branches in Glasgow, Edinburgh and Dundee, and in 1928 the *Sindacato Commercianti Italiani* (Italian Commercial Syndicate) was established. At about the same time the *Collegio dei Parrucchieri Italiani* (College of Italian Hairdressers) was set up in Glasgow. Various cultural associations were also formed, most notably the *Dante Alighieri* society in 1936. On the political front there were other more portentous developments.

In 1923, a year after Mussolini came to power in Italy, a branch of the Italian fascist movement was established in Glasgow comprising mainly members of the war veterans' associations (*Associazione Nazionale Combattenti* and the *Nastro Azzurro*) and some of the wealthier Italian businessmen. According to press accounts of the time fascist meetings held in Glasgow and Edinburgh in the 1920s regularly attracted large audiences. These meetings were social and political gatherings and it was not uncommon, for instance, to find members of the Roman Catholic hierarchy and the Italian Consulate in attendance as well as local dignitaries. In some cases meetings were specifically arranged to coincide with Roman Catholic holidays: for example, the annual reunion of the 'Italian fascisti' was held on August 15th, the Feast of the Day of the Assumption. Most Italians regarded 'the 15th' as the big social event in their year, as described here by a teenager of the time.

Opening of new hall and sale of work, Italian Fascists. The Italian Consul, Sen. Fronchetti, is right of centre.

"There always used to be a big picnic to celebrate the fifteenth of August and it was really a good day. Every year the Glasgow Italians, the Dundee Italians, the Edinburgh Italians all got together at some place, some big park, maybe it would be Alva or Stirling or somewhere. We used to have great fun—lots of food and games, tug-of-war and races and things like that. It was really good."

Without doubt Mussolini and his extraordinary brand of fascism enjoyed some support from within the immigrant community. Unlike Mosley's 'black-shirts', the Italian fascists made little impact and there is a conspicuous lack of evidence of antagonism towards the Italians in the 1930s in spite of the growing threat of fascist power on the Continent. The change came with Mussolini's declaration of war on 10th June 1940.

In a night of violence and looting, anti-Italian riots broke out in a number of places including Glasgow, Edinburgh, Falkirk, Greenock, Port Glasgow and Irvine. In one of the most serious disturbances, in Edinburgh, the police had to make several baton charges to disperse a crowd, estimated at over 1,000, which had gathered in Leith Walk. Few areas of Italian settlement were spared.

Marina Barsotti:
"I was in Glasgow when I heard it on the six o'clock news and my mother said, 'You'd better not go to Galston tonight, there might be trouble.' I thought it would be alright because it was just a wee village and nobody bothered us there. Well, this shop here in Wallace Street, a gang of hooligans broke the windows, they came in and over the counter to take the goods away, the likes of chocolate and so on. . . . It was a very frightsome night, certainly was, because you didn't know if you were going to get stoned to death or what was going to happen to you."

The scale and intensity of the violence of 10th June left the immigrant community bewildered and frightened. As Dominic Crolla put it, 'It seemed as if the work of fifty or sixty years had vanished into thin air.' Worse was to follow as the policy of internment of 'enemy aliens' was enforced. Fascists and non-fascists (including some German Jewish refugees) were treated alike.

Federico Pontiero:
"Och, they all started to hate me because I was an Italian. . . . I was up the public park one day

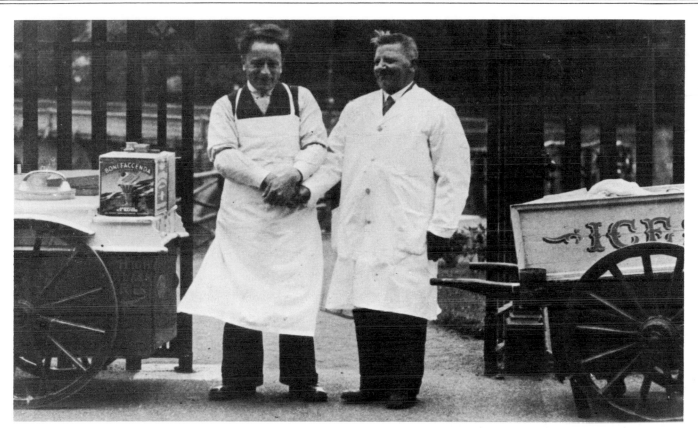

"Enemy Aliens"? Bothwell Bridge, c. 1920.

standin' wi' the barra' and this man, he says, 'Get away with that barra,' he says, 'you and Mussolini.' There was a gentleman standin' just beside me and he says [to him], 'Hallo, sir. What's the idea o' you tellin' him "Mussolini"? What has he got to do with Mussolini?' I thought that man had done a great thing and I appreciate that man's spoken for me. You see, I wasna' a political, I wasna' interested in politic at all. . . . That night the war broke out [10th June 1940] my wife, she had a baby dying o' pneumonia. Well the police came up the house, it was about eleven o'clock, and they start to look about and they says, 'You'll need to come with us.' I says, 'I don't know nothing about politic, I've been in Cambuslang most o' my days.' But anyway they took me up the jail and of course I broke doon because my wean was dyin'. The next day the wean died and the priest and the doctor came and they asked the Inspector if they would let me home for five minutes. He said 'No'. So they took us away to Milton Bridge and then from there to the Isle of Man."

Mrs D'Agostino:
"They interned most of the men, some went to the Isle of Man, some were sent to Canada, others to Australia. It was just a nightmare really. They took my brothers and one was only eighteen months when he came here. It was very sad because most of them didn't know anything about politics or fascism or anything, even the ones who belonged to the Fascist Club. It was just a social club which, unfortunately, was called the Fascist Club."

Dominic Crolla:
"Many Italians lost their lives on the *Arandora Star* which was going to Canada with a lot of British troops, German prisoners-of-war and Italians on board. I lost my own father on that ship, yes, the *Arandora Star* torpedoed by a German submarine. I myself was interned in Canada for nearly three years. We were with German prisoners-of-war on the boat and they were singing all the way over, singing that Britain was 'kaputt' and that the war would end very soon. We, on the other hand, about 300 of us who had been in Scotland for years, were all sad with long faces having been separated from our families and not knowing where we were going. . . ."

Few Italians were interned for the duration of the war unless they were Class 'A' internees, i.e. aliens who represented 'a potential security risk'. Members of this category were deported to Italy after the war. Most of the Scottish Italians had returned home by 1944 and within a few years the community was functioning once again on normal lines. Trade slowly began to improve and in some areas there were unexpected benefits.

Dominic Crolla:
"It wasn't a very successful business in these days [1930s] because people didn't know anything about spaghetti, wine or olive oil. It only dealt with Italian customers and with Italians who had small shops. . . . But after the war it was a huge success because British soldiers had been in Italy, tasted the

Mr Dominic Crolla and the staff of Valvona and Crolla Ltd., 1981.

spaghetti, tasted Italian food, some had been in India and tasted curry, some had been in France and Germany. When they all came back they wanted a change in their kitchen, hence the prosperity, the slow prosperity of Valvona and Crolla Ltd. . . . We were the only ones in Edinburgh at that time from whom they could purchase all these nice goods.''

The post-war years witnessed a new wave of immigrants, particularly after 1951 when the Government introduced the Bulk Recruitment Scheme in an attempt to compensate for the acute shortage of native labour in industries such as mining, steel-making and farming. Few Italians remained in these occupations once their contract was completed.

Mrs Lucchesi:
"Italy was very down at that time and the only way that they [Italians] could come over here was to do four years on the farms. After that they were free to take on any work they wanted. The women, they could come over if they were doing domestic work in hospitals or somewhere like that. There was quite a big community here, in fact in Galston they called it 'Little Italy' because right round the farms there was an awful lot of Italians. But after the four years they started getting shops through other Italians telling them there's a shop going to be let and so on. . . .''

Mr Ioannone:
"The farm I went to, it was just like slavery the way ye work there. The Scotchman, the boss, had a two son. All the job they no want to do, I had to do. When I'd overtime to do they just paid me two shillings an hour when everybody else a paid three

shillings or four shillings an hour! After the four years, after that, I start a myself a business, I started with the ice-cream van and after a couple of years wi' the fish and chips and now I have this wee grocery business.''

Unlike the pre-war period the migration from Italy in the 1950s and 1960s was on a massive scale: nearly 150,000 immigrants arrived in Britain between 1948 and 1968. As the Census returns show, however, only a tiny proportion of this number settled in Scotland and it is significant that in terms of the origins of the immigrants the composition of the community remains largely unaltered. A recent study of the present-day Italian community (by Ms Terri Colpi) has revealed that 90 per cent of the Italians in Glasgow came from the Garfagnana district of Lucca, while 80 per cent of those living in Edinburgh have connections with Picinisco in Frosinone province. The close-knit nature of the community, however, which was so powerful a feature of the early days, is gradually being weakened by integration and assimilation.

Mrs Lucchesi:
"The younger generation don't want to work late at night and they're just not interested in fish and chips. Although I still have the shop I have to let it out because my family are not interested. . . .
Today it's different. My family, we all married Italians, now my children instead, well my son, he's a teacher, he married a Scotch girl, a teacher, and my daughter married a local Scotch boy.''

Dominic Crolla:
"Well, it's losing a bit because of the inter-marriage. And it's losing a little because as the

more years pass, the more we're being absorbed into the ways of Scottish life. There's nothing more inevitable than that."

Mrs D'Agostino:

"Well, what I call the new immigrants, they're quite a new breed altogether. They are so entirely different from us that we have very little in common really. This doesn't mean to say that one is better than the other . . . but I think we have acquired a lot of British tastes, British habits. We like our freedom, we don't like to work after a certain hour, we enjoy living a little more gracious life. They're not interested in gracious living, only in acquiring. They're very hard working, I shudder at the work they do because I can remember having done something on the same lines when I was very young and I would hate to go back to that life. To me it's not living, it's just merely existing."

As in the past, most newcomers find employment in the catering trades in the 'pizzarias' and 'spaghetti houses' that have become so popular in the last decade or so. Few settle here permanently and it is partly because of this constant flow of new blood into the community that a strong sense of national identity remains. Other factors are also important, such as the increasing frequency of visits to relatives and friends in Italy and, perhaps equally important, a growing awareness among members of the community that their language and culture ought to be preserved.

Dr Franchi:

"In the last fifteen to twenty years there has been a great movement to keep this link alive. The *Dante Alighieri* society have a number of thriving branches and their forte is simply the spreading of Italian ideals and Italian culture. There are the Saturday morning classes in Edinburgh and Glasgow to teach the young ones exclusively Italian and Italian culture. And every year there is a conference organised, an Italian conference, and this is for the young people to rediscover their origins and to stay together for a few days not only socially but culturally as well."

As in all immigrant groups there will be some who will willingly and quickly adopt the culture and customs of their new 'homeland'. Some will remain indifferent to it and others will try to retain their original identity.

Dominic Crolla:

"Well, I've noticed it in my own family where my oldest girl, she's been to Italy with us on holiday and she loves Italy and came back and wanted to study Italian, whereas my youngest one, she knows nothing about Italy. . . . In the Argentine Games I remember we were all shouting for Italy and my wife was crying when Holland beat Italy 2-1 and my little girl, Carla, she was crying because

A young Federico Pontiero.

Scotland had been beaten. I don't want to go through that experience of the World Cup again!"

Clearly, in having a sense of national or cultural identity there is a security, a sense of belonging, an attachment, which meets an important human need. However, the search for an identity has its problems and as Federico Pontiero suggests, in a statement full of eloquence and honesty, perhaps the real search should be for social justice.

Federico Pontiero:

"Who can prove you are a Scots or he's an Italian? Nobody can prove what nationality we have. I mean the Romans, they occupied London for how many years? They occupied Britain for 400 years and how many children's been born in that time? What are they then? To me every people's the same, and I mean every person in this world has the right to live where he wants. This is God's land, it's a God's land for everybody, whether you're black or white or dark or whatever you are."

MURDOCH RODGERS

Mungo Mackay & the Green Table

Mungo Mackay and his Green Table may not have been unique in the Scottish coal industry during the half century before nationalisation in 1947, but he and his system of industrial and social control earned a notoriety among miners even in coalfields beyond the Lothians. In the Newtongrange area of Midlothian such a lasting impression has been left by Mackay's dominant personality and autocratic paternalism that today, forty years after his death, some older villagers are said still to believe 'Mungo's no' deid yet'.

Mackay, born in 1867, was not a Midlothian but an Ayrshire man. He had begun work as a mining engineer at Auchinleck Colliery before moving to Polton pit, Midlothian, about 1894. Coal mining was by then of course a very old industry in the Lothians. The monks of Newbattle Abbey, evidently the earliest miners in Scotland, were digging coal on the banks of the South Esk river from the thirteenth century until the Reformation. The Marquesses of Lothian, employing colliers as serfs until the Act of Emancipation in 1799, worked the coal around Newbattle and Newtongrange until the later nineteenth century. Then the Lothian Coal Company, formed in 1860 and expanded in 1890, took over production. This company, whose chief director James A. Hood was said to be a millionaire, was only one of half-a-dozen leading coal companies in the Lothians. They included the Arniston Coal Company, Edinburgh Collieries Ltd. and the Niddrie and Benhar Coal Company. With the growth of the export trade in coal and developments in technology, including greater mechanisation, mining in Midlothian began to develop at a much faster pace in the late nineteenth century. The opening of the Lady Victoria pit at Newtongrange in 1890 by the Lothian Coal Company marked the beginning of modern mining in the county. Thus Mungo Mackay's arrival in the district four years later more or less coincided with this 'take-off' of the industry.

Mackay soon became agent and general manager of the Lothian Coal Company and then in 1927 a director. He managed the three pits at or around Newtongrange, where the company's head office was situated—the Lady Victoria, Lingerwood and East-houses. Late in his career, after the death of his fellow-manager Mr Hamilton of Rosewell, Mackay was responsible also for the colliery there, known as Whitehill pit, and for the nearby Polton pit. Mackay died in 1939 and is buried in Newbattle cemetery.

Even in an industry hardly noted in those times for kindly or sympathetic relations between the private coal companies and the miners, Mungo Mackay's paternalism and autocracy were remarkable.

Opposite: Mungo Mackay in Masonic regalia.

Authoritarian colliery managers were then one of many occupational hazards that miners had to face daily, but none of his contemporaries appears to have earned quite so much notoriety among Scots miners as did Mackay. In the West Lothian shale mines, for instance, managers like Bryson of Pumpherston and A. C. Thomson of Oakbank attempted to discipline and control their miners both at work and in the more remote villages, but neither succeeded to the extent that Mackay did further east. His techniques of industrial and social control, his ruthlessness in applying them, and his relative success, are rather reminiscent of the old West of Scotland coalmasters recently so well discussed by Alan B. Campbell in his history of the Lanarkshire miners in the century preceding 1874. Mackay could be seen as a survival from an earlier and harder epoch, a kind of early twentieth-century Baird of Gartsherrie.

Tommy Kerr:
"Ah stayed in East Lothian and ah started in the pits in 1926 frae ah wis a lad leavin' the school. Now miners in the Lothians area used to talk about 'Up the braes'—Newtongrange and that area—in whispers. They used to say, 'If there's one place that ah widna like tae work it's up in the area where this man Mackay has the control and the terror struck in the hearts o' the workmen'."

Mackay's reputation spread also in Fife. Some militant miners there, victimised after the 1926 lock-out, sought work in the pits at Newtongrange, no doubt keeping their views well hidden. But on their first pay-day they became merry in the pub and began to sing strike ditties and *The Red Flag*. They were summoned before Mungo Mackay and his Green Table and were back in Fife by nightfall.

The authority that Mackay exercised in Newtongrange, and his personality, are recalled by one of his wages clerks who worked under him for many years in the 1920s and '30s.

James Reid:
"Mungo was a well-built man, about six feet, quite a good lookin' man, moustache. But he had an unfortunate way of speaking to people, always startin' wi' [cough] clearing his throat. Now ah may be biased but he always gave me the impression that I was beneath him. He must have given the miners the verra same, must have. Ah can't tell ye any funny stories about him because ah think he was absolutely devoid o' humour. Ah can't remember ever seein' him smile. But he was the type that demonstrated to the full 'master and man'. There were a class which he belonged to, and there

Office staff, Lothian Coal Company, c. 1930. James Reid is top right.

were a class that ah belonged tae. And ah found then although ah was only a young man that if you were a surveyor you were everything, if you were a wages clerk you were a nothing."

There is no evidence that Mackay ever became a particularly wealthy man. His rise to the position of supreme control that he maintained in and around the villages of Newtongrange, Gorebridge, Birkenside, Arniston, Rosewell, Poltonhall, and Bonnyrigg, seems to have been based very much on his professional skill. Opinion is unanimous that Mungo Mackay was an outstandingly able mining engineer.

Tommy Kerr:
"Ah'm gaun tae pay him a compliment, and it's against the grain. But bein' a miner and aware o' what is essential in minin' is efficiency—both for safety and other reasons—ah would say that Mackay must have been a first-class minin' engineer. If Mackay hadn't played the part that he did in pursuin' a line of road-making in Lady Victoria in all probability Lady Victoria, followin' the War, would hae been shut much earlier than 1981, because when the boom for coal come about the handy coal was taken from the main roadsides and other places and Mackay's roadways stood the test. In fact, it's been often said that he used to have a three-foot stick that he could hold above his head and if that stick touched any part of the roadway, instructions were immediately given tae get it heightened. So that gives ye an idea o' the man's ability as a minin' engineer."

Much of Mackay's success in disciplining and controlling the miners of the Lothian Coal Company arose from the fact that the company's pits were run on the contracting system.

Pat Flynn:
"The system o' contractin' wis, there were one man used to go to the bosses in the pit and say, 'Ah'll do this for ye.' And he got a price fur minin' coal. He'd probably say he'd gie ye 5d. or 10d. a ton. And this chap wid hire other people—that's the contractin'. So ma dad, he wis hired."

Miners, and their unions, were generally hostile to the contracting system and sought its abolition.

James Reid:
"At that time, a man that was on the face, if he worked his five shifts—there were no overtime paid—would be lucky if he had £3 a week. Whereas you, as contractor, was probably takin' home £30. Mungo Mackay believed in this system, which is long gone now, because it was puttin' the workin' man against the workin' man."

Newtongrange Main Street and Picture House, 1920s.

The miners' union in the Lothians—the Mid and East Lothian Miners' Association, which was a purely county union like those in all other Scots coalfields before the 1940s—was not very strong or militant. It was too small, and unemployment among miners, as among other workers, was usually too great for the union to wield much power. It seems to have found no effective answer to the tactics and practices of Mungo Mackay.

Tommy Kerr:

"He tolerated the Trade Union movement but that was all that he did. John Rutherford was a checkweigher appointed by the men. On many occasions Mungo Mackay used the psychology o' imposition, and he would ask him up, the likes o' a trade union official like John, to go to the office and he would keep him waitin' and waitin' and waitin'. This was one o' his methods o' gettin' the first blow in in any negotiations that might have to take place."

As far as the wages clerks of the Lothian Coal Company were concerned, Mackay resolutely opposed any attempt by them to form a union.

James Reid:

"Ah didn't personally try to start a union but we started to talk about it through a wages clerk who went off the rails, started cheatin', and he was found out. Well, he had started two years after me

and of course in the court case his salary came out and he had £1 something more than I had. And we got our heads together. For instance, ah didn't know what Joe Soaps on ma left hand, or John Broon on ma right, had. Ye never knew anybody's wages. There were no scales nor nothing, and of course ah said, 'Look, it's high time we were doin' something.' And ah was told wi' the Chief Wages Clerk: 'You try, or any o' you try, to form a union and you'll be replaced. Period. You'll be replaced.' So that we were actually cowed. Now anybody listenin' to ma story will say, 'Well, why did they stick that?' Well, at that time—we're approachin' it now—there were over three million unemployed. Ah had no degrees, ah'd left the public school at fourteen, ah had nothing. And a job was a job. And that's the sole reason."

Some of the Lothian Coal Company miners, not surprisingly, felt themselves to be in a state of semi-serfdom, little freer than the old Newbattle miners in the times before the Emancipation of 1799. Mackay's power seemed to many to be not merely unchallenged but unchallengeable. He seemed to have complete freedom to practice a policy of divide and rule. Among the office staff the application of this policy took the form of favouritism.

James Reid:

"If ye was on the Staff, ye could get a bag o' sticks, if ye had the right side of his face, a beautiful big bag o' chopped sticks to keep ye goin'. Ah never got sticks. Another difference he made with the Staff was when you were married and ye paid rent and rates. Now at that time it was seven shillings and 1/9d. rates, year after year, there was no jumpin' like what there is nowadays. Well, ye suddenly found out when ye started talkin' seriously about tryin' to all be equal, that one person was payin' seven shillin's, but not the rates. Another person was payin' the full thing. Another favoured person was rent-free. Now seven shillin's and 1/9d. in those days was really something. Then it came to the coal. Some had free coal. Others paid fifteen and ninepence, plus the cartage. In other words, he set the Staff one against another just the same as he did with the miner by his contractin' system."

Of course other private coal companies also operated the contracting system. But this method of dividing and ruling the miners Mackay characteristically extended from their place of work to their place of residence—from the pits to the villages. Some of the contractors and some other miners and villagers acted as spies and informers for Mackay not only in the pits but also in the miners' rows in Newtongrange and the other villages owned or dominated by the Lothian Coal Company.

Tommy Kerr:
"If any organisation was set up he used to query it and find out what its intentions was, and every step was taken to ensure that he was well informed. The contractors of course were the first line o' his defence. They got inflated wages and they acted as spies."

James Reid:
"Ah don't think ah ever once in ma life saw him walkin' through the village. 'Cause he didn't need to, it was like the coal face—he had his informants who told him what was goin' on in the village. The company policeman knew everythin' that went on in the village. The result is he took it up the stair to Mungie Mackay. There were a head timekeeper and another man, who I shall leave nameless, and actually they were just go-betweens. Everythin' that they heard went up the stair to Mungo Mackay. With the result that, as the years went on, he ruled like a king. He really ruled like a king in this village. It's a known fact that a man could have a row on a Saturday night, wi' maybe a pint in him, and got into a wee bit fight, and on Monday he was up in front o' Mungo Mackay because somebody went up and told him. He could actually know that your next door neebour and his wife had a row. It was amazing. You talk aboot Gestapo. It was really good, it was really good."

Tommy Kerr, a militant trade unionist living and working in East Lothian, had no personal contact with Mackay and did not move to Midlothian to work in the pits there until several years after Mackay's death. Nonetheless:

"Ah was aware o' his power over the workers and his representation of the Lothian Coal Company. There's no doubt if ever there were a reputation that could make money for the employers he was the one, at the expense of the employees.
"The powers o' Mackay was so great that if a man didnae attend his work he could phone the local Dean Tavern and instruct the barman: 'This man's not, if he comes in, he's not to receive any drink. He's not to get a pint.' "

Mackay's attempts to recruit informers were not, however, always successful.

Tommy Thomson:
"Well, on Thursday, ah come up and handed in ma tokens, and the rattle, knock on the window, [they] said, 'You're wanted up the stair at four o'clock.' Ah said to maself, 'What have you done already?' When ah went in Mr Mackay's was a long face. 'Tom,' he says, 'ah've a job for you.' Ah says, 'Oh, what's that?' He says, 'I want you to go to Lingerwood pit as an oversman.' Ah said, 'I'll hae tae consider it.' He says, 'Here, where did you get all your experience?' Ah said, 'From ma father and you.' He said, 'Because ah've been hearing good reports about you.' He said, 'Ah've never yet appointed an oversman that's come to me without tellin' the tale. So,' he says, 'ah want to have a check on everything that's in Lingerwood.' 'Well, Mr Mackay,' ah said, 'if that's the case you're no' gettin' me.' He said, 'Come on now, away go home and think it over for a fortnight.' But ah never would take the oversman's job."

Mackay's control over the miners both at work and in the villages, particularly at Newtongrange and Rosewell, was based on the ownership by the Lothian Coal Company of all or most of the houses in which the miners and their families lived. One aspect of his paternalism was his insistence that the miners must keep tidy the gardens of their tied houses.

Alexander Trench:
"If Mr Mackay had been livin' today this village would ha' been a hunder per cent better than what it is, especially the older houses. In these days if you didn't dig your garden there was a man sent down to dig your garden for you and you paid for it. Mr Mackay used to have a walk round himself round the houses to see if the gardens were being looked after. It was a model village all through Mr Mackay. He seen that it was a model village."

Tommy Thomson:
"He used to come down through the village,

Lady Victoria pit.

The Collier's Song

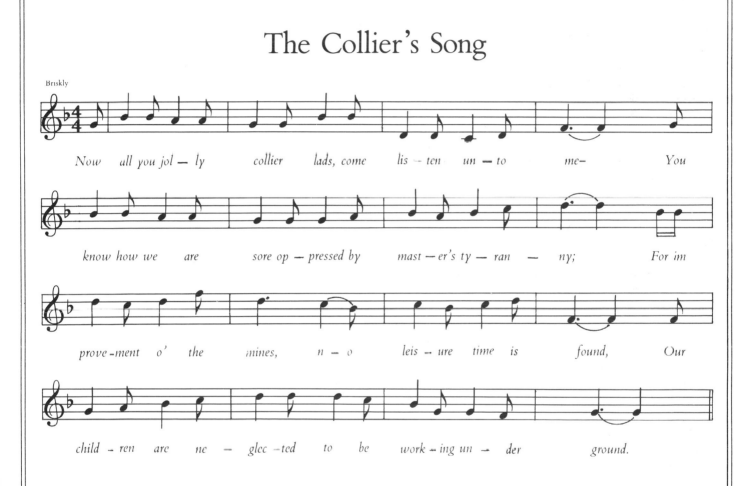

Now all you jol—ly collier lads, come lis—ten un—to me— You

know how we are sore op—pressed by mast—er's ty—ran—ny; For im

prove—ment o' the mines, n—o leis—ure time is found, Our

child—ren are ne—glec—ted to be work—ing un—der ground.

Our masters are tyrannical and that they must confess,
They overtax their workmen and do them sore oppress;
No other occupation so dangerous can be found,
We cannot call our lives our own while working underground.

The sailor he does plough the main and perils does go through,
But he sees the danger coming which a collier cannot do;
With fallen roofs and fire damp the records can be found,
How hundreds yearly lost their lives by working underground.

Frae Newtongrange and Arniston, frae Polton and Gorebrig,
Frae Birkenside tae Lasswade, Cockpen and Bonnyrigg;
Frae Rosewell tae Newbattle the Lothian men a' say,
We're no the likes o' ither men that works an eight hours day.

Better quality housing occupied by contractors in Newtongrange.

walking with his stick, to see how everything was lookin'. And down near the bottom pub there wis a man wi' the name o' Toshie Moffat. Toshie couldna be bothered doin' his garden at any time. So Mr Mackay sent for Toshie to come up to the office one day, and he said to him: 'Toshie, yer gairden's a disgrace tae the raw. What are ye gaun tae dae aboot it?' Toshie looked at Mungie and he said, 'Mr Mackay, ye havenae seen ma gairden right because,' he said, 'there are tatties planted in ma gairden.' 'Oh, no, no, Toshie,' he says, 'they're no' tatties planted in your gairden.' He said, 'The tatties,' he says, 'that you're talkin' about are all long gress.' "

To punish indiscipline by miners down the pits or in the villages Mackay, or his henchmen, sometimes threatened or imposed that traditional weapon of coal-owners—eviction from company housing.

James 'Treacle' Moffat:
   "Mungo Mackay wisna feared tae tell ye if ye done onythin' wrong—'Ah'll put ye out the house.' Ye had tae dae what ye wis telt—or else. His heid man as manager of the Lady was Willie Kerson. An' the under-manager wis Peter Dixon. And they telt ye, 'Ye'll do what ye're told—or else.' An' he says to me one day: 'Ye'll do what ye're told or ah'll put ye out your house.' So ah says, 'Well, ye'll just have to put ez out the house,' ah says, 'ah've a good home tae go tae.' 'Aye,' he says, 'if ye gang back to yer faither and mither we'll pit them out the house too.' "

Pat Flynn:
   "Now I've heard stories such as Mackay, he'd send for this man, Joe Thomson or whoever, and say, 'Hello, Joe, come in here.' Of course, ye'd go in wi' your hat under your elbow and stand verra much to attention and don't speak until you're spoken to—almost in front of the Crime Squad. And he'd say, 'Ah see you've a son leavin' school on Friday.' And the chap would say, 'Yes, ah hiv, yes, and ah've got a job for him as an apprentice'—ah don't know what it wis, a joiner, plumber, whatever. 'Ah,' he says, 'but ah've got a job here in the pit for him.' And he says, 'But ah'd like ma laddie tae try and dae somethin' better than the pits and ah've got him an apprenticeship.' 'Oh, no, ye'd better bring him up here.' And the chap says, 'Well, ah'd like him to be an apprentice.' And the end of the conversation [Mackay says] 'Either bring him up, start him on Monday, or bring up the keys o' the house.'
   "Well, ye can understand the position o' this man. What's he gonnae do? So thereby another miner, not by choice by any means, ended up in the pits. And that's the way it worked, that's the way his system went on. You can imagine the power that this man had."

Miners' housing, Newtongrange.

An elder in the Church of Scotland and first Right Worshipful Master of the Newtongrange Freemasons, Mackay is said to have used both religion and freemasonry in building up his control over the miners.

Tommy Kerr:

"Oh, aye, he was a leadin' figure in the Church. But he was a fly man, he was never sectarian. Ah believe that his association wi' Roman Catholicism was pretty well known in the locality. Ah believe he was friendly wi' the local priests and other people and he conferred wi' them. Many people that ah know in Newtongrange and in the locality got promotion as a consequence o' bein' seen in the church by Mackay."

Pat Flynn:

"Ah wis born in Rosewell. Ma dad was Irish, and he came across to Scotland it must ha' been in the early 'twenties or maybe before that. There seemed to be a hell of a lot of Irish people in Rosewell. A lot o' people referred to it as 'Little Ireland'. Ah often wonder as time goes by why were so many Irish people congregated in the one place? And ah wonder was there so many Protestants congregated in the other half i' the Lothian Coal Company's set-up, namely Newtongrange? An' ah often wonder tae masel, wis this a policy o' Mungie Mackay? Or wis it a policy o' the Lothian Coal Company? As an

individual, ah never heard any concrete evidence to this fashion, but ah wonder, wis he tryin' to divide and conquer? That's what's at the back o' ma head."

Such methods of control, practised by Mackay for about forty years until his retirement in the 1930s, were made possible partly by the deference shown toward him personally and his system by many of the employees of the Lothian Coal Company and their families. This deference may have been to some extent an outcome of many generations of subjection of local miners, stretching back to the centuries when they were the serf-colliers of the Marquesses of Lothian. Whatever the reasons deference certainly oiled the wheels of Mackay's system.

At Rosewell, a few miles west of Newtongrange, Mungo Mackay's writ ran but there it was enforced not so much by himself as by his fellow Lothian Coal Company manager, Mr Hamilton.

Pat Flynn:

"Mr Hamilton was the manager o' Rosewell or Whitehill Colliery. And in the workshops, ye know, the blacksmith's shop, the engineerin' shop, the electric shop, if he happened to be comin', they used tae hae a signal which went: 'SSSSSHH SSSSSH'—which meant, 'Get workin'', or 'Get oot the road', or 'Get lost'. So this went on for years. Every time they heard this noise they used to scatter, ye know, if they were talkin' aboot a game o' football, or dogs, or pigeons, or whatever, they used to scatter. This chap, Mr Hamilton, who was the manager, died. And he lived in a house a few hundred yards up from the colliery. And on the day he was gettin' buried the hearse was passin' by the workshops, so they were peerin' out, lookin', lookin' at this great man passin' in this coffin, and says, 'Oh, look at him, oh.' And all o' a sudden somebody came to the door and went 'SSSSSHH SSSSSH'. And they all scattered. And here's the man goin' by in his coffin—and they were still terrified for him."

Mackay's autocracy even extended to the Newton-grange pipe band.

James Reid:
"He sent for me one day and he said, 'Reid, I want you to be secretary and treasurer of the pipe band.' I said, 'Pipe band?' He said, 'Yes, it's starting this week, and I want them on the right lines. We'll get permission to take a penny off.' So I had to collect the pennies [from the miners' pay packets] and report every month to him. Then he came to the choosing of the tartan, and he went through Maclean, MacDuff, Mackenzie, MacGregor, Mackay. And he stopped at Mackay, naturally. And he says, 'How would that look?' It wis a hellish tartan: it was yellow, and yellow, and more yellow, what ah recollect. Of course it was all the same what ah said. 'Aye, we'll have the Mackay tartan for the band.' Well, this actually happened. I had the order made up; it was an Edinburgh firm of kiltmakers. And this morning Mungo Mackay sent for me at half-past nine and he says, 'I've changed my mind. Ye'd better cancel it and get the Royal Stuart.' 'Oh, my God,' I says. I had everything written out: Mackay. The order was already in the post box. Ah had to belt down that road to the post office and I had to plead with the postmaster, 'Look, you've got to open the box and let me get that letter out or I'm shot, I'm as dead as a door nail.' The postmaster knew me and opened up the box and gave me the letter back and I went up and rewrote it for the Royal Stuart tartan."

It was at the Green Table that Mungo Mackay, like some medieval lord of the manor among his serfs, meted out 'justice'. The Green Table was a large table intended for the laying-out of colliery plans.

James Reid:
"Well, he had a fairly large room, and actually all that was in it was some minin' books and this big table, green-covered. And he sat behind and you when you were summoned you were not asked to sit. You stood in front o' the Green Table."

Many miners summoned before the Green Table suffered palpitations.

Alexander Trench:
"Mr Mackay sent for you, to 'go up the stair'. And when you knew you were goin' 'up the stair', it was no joke, you knew what you were goin' tae face. And you had to be clean, a collar and tie on, and go up and see Mr Mackay. And he was very efficient and verra fair, askin' the questions, 'Why did you not do this, why did . . .?' and you had to answer. If you didn't, he fairly rapped you over the fingers for not doin' it properly."

Mackay never presided alone at the Green Table. Always beside him he would place the Lothian Coal Company policeman. This policeman was one of Mackay's chief lieutenants in maintaining his control, industrial and social, over the miners.

Tommy Kerr:
"Ah believe that the policeman were as much subservient to the will o' Mackay as any workmen. The men used the expression in the pits, 'Is you for the Green Table? Some man, eh? Ye're goin' up there to get a bit belabourin'?' The company policeman was only the tool that was used as a psychological threat to the men. Ah never knew o' any violence takin' place any time."

Sometimes Mackay also required the presence of additional henchmen at the Green Table, such as under-managers or pit oversmen. But always he alone did the talking. He alone made all the pronouncements on charges, evidence, and passed sentence on accused miners.

James 'Treacle' Moffat:
"Aye, ma powny run away and when oo went up tae the splint mine the oversman, Jimmy Long, was stan'in wi' the powny. He says, 'What's the powny dae'in up here itsel'?' An' ah says, 'It run away.' It could run harder than me. 'Aw?' he says, 'ye have to see Mr Mackay aboot that.' So ah was sent for. They put a line on your token: 'Gaun up and see Mr Mackay at four o'clock or half-past four.' When ah went up he says, 'What have you been doin'?' And ah says, 'Nothin' that ah ken o'.' So he says, 'You must have been daein somethin'.' Ah says, 'It must be about ma powny runnin' away.' 'Aye,' he says, 'that's right.' So oo had a wee bit blether back and forrit and he says, 'Jist tae learn ye a lesson,' he says, 'oo'll fine ye ten bob but ye'll get it back in three month on your good behaviour.' So ah wis good behaviour for the next three month and ah got back ma ten bob."

Sentences imposed by Mackay at the Green Table included fines—sometimes collective—and of course dismissal from the company's employment, which included loss of a tied house.

Alexander Trench:
"We got fined a pound losing two grease cups.

Lady Victoria pit bottom, c. 1900.

Now grease cups were on machinery and they must have got lost some way, with the turning and the moving about as often. And we lost two o' them. So we were fined a pound. But that pound came off the pool. It wasn't one person that lost that pound, it come off the pool where there were about maybe twenty men included in. But that was one of the things, if you lost anything you had to pay for it. You got the choice what hospital you sent the fines to. Most o' them went to Edinburgh Royal Infirmary."

James Reid:
"Now it was genuine, because the next week in your payline you got a receipt from the Edinburgh Royal Infirmary, to thank you for your £1. But the poond at these days happened to be one-third of your total week's wage, which seemed a bit hard to me."

The surviving older generation of Newtongrange and district miners, and their families, who lived under Mungo Mackay's regime until his death in 1939, appear to divide largely into two groups. There are those who respected or even admired him and his system; and those who, with varying degrees of intensity, did not. Only a few take up a middle position.

James 'Treacle' Moffat:
"Well, he was a kind o' bad man an' he was a kind o' guid man at times. If ye went up tae see him, if he sent for ye to gin up, he wid argue wi' ye an' he wid grant ye your side o' the story if he thocht ye wis right."

Mrs Mary McLaren:
"He wis a hard man but right to the core. He got his way, whether you liked it or no'. He was a good man tae this village in every way. If a man was sent to a job it had to be done. And ye never heard o' strikes in thae days wi' Mungie Mackay. He wis a genuine man, a right good man."

John Telfer:
"Well, Mr Mackay was very well liked in the village. He was strict but he was good."

James Reid:
"You'll get people in this village who yearn for the old days, you know: 'Aw, if Mungo Mackay was back; this village is gaun tae hell now.' Maybe so, but ye can put your foot on a man's neck jist a wee bit too hard, you know. That's what ah thought he did."

IAN MacDOUGALL

The Fisher Lassies

"It was all done for the love o' oor men folk. If we hadn't worked, they couldn't have sold their fish."

This was how Mrs Annie Sellings, now ninety years old, a herring gutter in her early years, summed up the commitment of the women of Scottish fishing communities to the herring industry of the late nineteenth and early twentieth centuries. Fisher girls grew up ready to learn and follow the trade of curing herring for the German and Russian markets. There was a boom in the export of salt herring to these countries from about 1870 to 1914 and these were prosperous times for the fisher people of Nairn and the North East. In their fast and versatile Zulu sail boats, later replaced by steam drifters, they caught huge quantities of herring for the eager and stable curing industry. With their new wealth many built good stone houses, bought fashionable clothes, had grand weddings, and generally enjoyed a high standard of living.

Before this, line fishing, with its endless and repetitive tasks which brought meagre financial reward, was the mainstay of fishing communities and provided only a hand to mouth existence. The lusty appetites of the German and Russian people for salt herring caused a dramatic change in the lives of those who followed the fishing trade, and ushered in a welcome period of hope, happiness and financial security.

From my own town of Nairn, about thirty drifters left in their seasons to fish the herring grounds off Fraserburgh, Wick, Shetland, Stornoway, Yarmouth and Lowestoft. Teenage girls and young unmarried women, mainly relatives of the fishermen, followed soon after, to gut and pack the herring, having previously been engaged by curers for the work. They were provided with accommodation and paid by the barrel. Living conditions were primitive, the pay was miserable and the work exhausting. In spite of all that, however, those who still survive, and most are now very old, in their youth eagerly looked forward to and greatly enjoyed the gutting, especially in Shetland. They loved the independence and comradeship of living away from home in huts with their friends, in charge of their own domestic arrangements, experiencing a temporary period of communal living. It was like a working holiday.

The fishing industry, like farming in the days before mechanisation, required the involvement of the whole family, and women were expected to play their full part. They helped with the line fishing in their home ports by digging up bait, redding and baiting lines, splitting, salting and smoking fish, and finally travelling around the countryside bartering or selling them. When salt herring were being exported on a large scale from the British Isles, it was natural that the women should transfer their energies to supporting this lucrative market. The process of curing was an important related activity which could only be

Above: The steam drifter 'Glenerne', owned by the author's family. Opposite: Two Nairn gutting crews, Lerwick, c. 1885.

successfully operated by teams of women workers and they migrated in hundreds from their homes to large ports all around the coast, to deal with the continuous and massive catches of herring being landed by their menfolk.

William Stewart:

"By the end of the eighteen hundreds there was something like two hundred boats of all sorts and sizes pursuing the herring fishing in Lossiemouth. As the years went by the herring fishery opened in other areas, but boats started tae get bigger and then went further afield so that in Lossiemouth the fishermen started tae go other places—Stornoway, Lerwick, Ireland, Lowestoft, Yarmouth, Grimsby— wherever the herring was to be found, the fishermen followed in their sail boats.

"At the turn of the century came the steam and in Lossiemouth again, steam gradually took over from sail. As the steam drifters emerged in large numbers from all ports, the herring fishing carried on to unprecedented scale.

"Goin' back to the early days o' herrin' fishin' there would never hae been the herrin' fishin' if it hadna been fur the fisher lassies tae gut the herrin'. And they came from all ports on the Moray Firth— Cromarty, Avoch, Findhorn, Helmsdale, Burghead, Hopeman, Lossie, Nairn, was well represented in the fisher lassies guttin' the herrin'. One wonders at times just how they survived. The conditions was so severe that they worked in, especially in the winter time, in places where snow was deep, the winds blowin', frost. Nevertheless, it was their bread and butter and more so, it was their husbands', fathers', and sons' bread and butter.

"In the nineteen hundreds there was something like, from Lossie alone, three hundred girls went to the guttin'. In Nairn there'd probably be half that number anyway; Burghead and Hopeman equally much about the same. Buckie, probably five or six hundred, Buckie and the district, and Fraserburgh about the same. And all in a', roond aboot these years, there must have been something like three thousand girls engaged in the guttin' industry."

A sum of money knows as arles, usually one pound was paid to the gutting crews as an earnest of their intention to work for the curer who engaged them. Before each fishing, representatives of different curers visited fishing towns to recruit girls for the work. They arranged themselves in threes, two gutters and a packer, and worked together, often for many seasons and in many places, until marriage broke up the partnership.

Mrs Isabella Stewart:

"The curer called and engaged ye, well asked ye, and then ye got yer crew, it was three in a crew. It

Isabella Stewart of Lossie, third from right, with her crew and coopers. Yarmouth, c. 1920.

wis piece work efter that, ye see, jist whatever
much barrels ye could fill. At that time, it was
sixpence for a barrel."

Miss Jean Bochel:
  "We looked forward to it. I suppose we were
like the gypsics, when it came to the time of year,
you just sorta, sorted up yer things and away."

  The Sumburgh Roost, the confluence of the Atlantic
Ocean and the North Sea, creates uncomfortable and
hazardous sailing conditions which were particularly
dreaded by the fisher girls forced to make the crossing
from Aberdeen to Lerwick for the gutting season.
Some were sick even at the thought of it, others were
dreadfully sick when on board. It gave my mother a
distaste for the sea which lasted all her life.

Miss Jean Bochel:
  "It was beyond description the boat, you
wouldna like tae see it. A lota sickness, a lota girls,
just the thought—there was a woman over there,
she died just last year, whenever she got the
telegram that she was leaving on Monday she would
be upstairs lookin' at the sea and she'd be sick
before she'd ever go away—just the thought of it
made them sick!
  "You just lay down where you saw a space,
that's all, very much steerage. I don't know how
many boats would have left Aberdeen to go to
Lerwick because they went by the Aberdeen Steam
Navigation Company and they had a lot of extra
boats on then and I don't know how many girls but
I'm sure there'd be two or three hundred in every
boat—exclusively fish workers at that time I'd
imagine."

Mrs Eveline Crockett:
  "The cattle that was taken aboard that ship was
far more taken care of than what we were. We
were on the deck and the crew was very sorry fur
us, they used tae put tarpaulins ower the top of us."

Miss Jean Bochel:
  "Everybody went down, they were very quiet,
everybody expected to be sick, but I was quite a
good sailor. You had to take your own food, we
didn't have any meals or anything there, we didn't
have very much money at the time, very poor. I
wouldn't have much in ma bag tae take fur eating.
And I was a good eater, I still am, and they'd all
start bein' sick—sick, I'd go all round their bags
and I'd be eatin' all their stuff! So one time coming
from Lerwick tae Aberdeen, you know how the
Captain comes to the top o' the gangway and sees
you all going ashore and he says, 'You over there,
you,' points his finger to me to come—and I, face
like a beetroot, didn't know what on earth I was
going to get a tellin' off for, I wasn't in the way o'
gettin' tellin' offs—and he says 'The next time you
come, take a nose bag, it would be far handier for

*Dressing up for the photographer was one of the first things the
girls did after settling in for the season. Fraserburgh, c. 1895.*

you!' He was seein' me go all round the people and
looking to see what was for to eat.
  "The Roost was a very bad—I was always
saying, 'Where's the Roost, [have] we passed it?'
[an old hand said] 'You come and ask me that
again,' she says, 'I'll hit ye!' On a calm day it
would still be rough."

  In Shetland the curers provided the gutting crews
with rent-free huts which were unfurnished apart from
bunk beds and an open fireplace. In the early days the
girls slept three to a bed and lived six to a hut. Their
wooden kists, brought from home filled with clothes
and domestic utensils, were used as tables and chairs in
the huts. Screens were put up at the windows, and a
'glory hole' curtained off for toilet purposes. All this
was completed on the first day so that the girls were
ready, if needed, to start gutting the next morning.

Mrs Eveline Crockett:
  "We had to walk two mile oot tae Gremista and
when we arrived at Gremista, the huts that we
were gaun intae wes full o' barrels. Fit we had tae
dae was empty the barrels oot o' the huts. Then
we'd tae take a pail o' water and scrub oot the huts
and make them liveable. The curers wasna
carin'—they wouldna care less. So therefore, we

Interior of a herring gutters' hut, in Shetland, with brick fireplace, wooden bunks and wallpapered walls.

went ben to wir hoosie and—it was a sorta home because we wis nine weeks there. Mind you it wasna like hame, but we made it [like home] and we had bunk beds and there was a hole there they ca'ed the glory hole—the glory hole could tell mony a tale ah'm tellin' ye! (laughs) Well it held mair than pots and pans mony a time, but never mind! (laughs) But never mind!"

Mrs Margaret Duthie:
"Ye'd tae take in water in pails from an outside tap ye know and put on pans of water ontae a coal fire, it was always a coal fire. And washing facilities—we'd a barrel o' water, rain water at the door, ye know, and of course, it was just the basin, we'd nuthin' else."

Mrs Isabella Stewart:
"You took your own dishes and mats and everything with ye, ye see, it was jist an empty hut."

Miss Jean Bochel:
"We'd have to paper or paint the place and then take an old chest, kists we called them, and that did for seats and that was our furniture. We used to take pictures with us and we'd leave them, and a mirror and we'd have vases and all sorts—and we'd to provide our own lamp—it was oil lighting we had."

Mrs Annie Finlayson:
"We took our own beds wi' us, chaff, a' oor own beds, our own cookin' utensils. No electric ovens

then nor gas cookers nor nothin', just the open fire. And we made just as good scones and pancakes then as you can do now."

Some girls left home at the age of fourteen to become gutters, usually in the company of older sisters or cousins. So close were neighbourly and family ties at the time that any young girl from the fishing community was warmly and affectionately regarded by the whole group and her welfare and progress became the concern of all. She was expected to 'learn by doing', getting some guidance and encouragement from experienced friends. Already used to many household tasks, mending nets, knitting, sewing, cooking and baiting lines, her fingers adapted in a very short time to the use of the sharp gutting knife and, quickly extracting the guts, she threw them into cougs, and the herring into tubs at the rate of one a second.

Miss Jean Bochel:
"Usually the foreman came and knocked at every door at five o'clock—'Get up, get up, get up.' One girl took a day on, and if it was your day on ye had tae get up and light the fire and boil the kettle, make a cuppa tea and bread and butter—no toast. And then we started work at six prompt and it was prompt—because one was vying with the other, ye see, ye couldna be late."

Mrs Margaret Duthie:
"I was a gutter and had all my fingers tied up, you know, and workin' the knife, pretty fast—ye had to. Oh, ye were self-taught. Ye were just thrown in the deep end, just had tae pick up a knife

Dressing injured hands at the Mission in Yarmouth.

and start away. But the men were there, the coopers, they were overseein' the work and they would tell ye ye went wrong, ye know. We were all green at the beginning and ye had tae buck up and make a name for yerself sort of thing, and I remember—bein' the youngest, some of them got married and I was left tae get in wi' the older ones, ye know, so I had tae work hard tae keep up with them because we were all number one, two and three crew, ye know, just went by yer barrels, how many barrels ye did in a day, whether you were number one crew or two, like that. And of course I didn't want tae let the side down, I had tae work hard.

"The good crews got goin' tae Ireland ye see. I just went to Fraserburgh one year. But it was always Lerwick, and then, over tae Ireland. We went from there one year to North Shields and then from there down to Yarmouth."

To protect their fingers from the knife working at high speed, the girls tied cotton cloths round their fingers. These were washed daily and the string skilfully secured by hands and teeth.

Miss Jean Bochel:
"We had oilskin skirts and we had kerchiefs on our heads and we tied our fingers with cotton cloths."

Mrs Annie Finlayson:
"Oh your fingers, you had to watch yer fingers,

had to be tied up and we got cotton, linen cloths ye know, ye know the flour bags, that the bakers had. Used tae buy them for about fourpence or threepence each, two o' them or three o' them kept us goin', and washed them and bleached them and tore it up in strips for yer fingers, that's how you'd keep your fingers. We'd tae keep them on all day, ye couldna take them off at lunchtime, you just washed your hands thoroughly in hot water. If it was festered, you put a bread poultice on it and sugar in the poultice. Bread poultice and sugar and put it to your finger if you had a festered hand and that cured it. There were no lance—you couldna get it lanced or any o' that sort o' thing, that cured it, nurse it and cured it and it just went away just then. And then you put on a thin cloth to keep it from the salt, and then ye were okay.

"Sometimes ye'd get a mackerel, you know, maybe if ye didna notice maybe grab your hands, and your finger could be pretty sore. But then there were what they called the Red Cross Hut there, what you call a Mission that ye went til if there was anything the matter, and got yer hands dressed which was very good. There was a nurse there, for dressing yer hands. But that was the only thing that was, watching yer hands, ye know. But ye see you were so quick, ye had tae be quick! Unless ye wanta work for no money at all ye had tae be quick ye see."

The hectic process of gutting and packing was interrupted throughout the day while crews carried their full tubs two at a time for rousing. Herring were partially salted in the farlins, but this more thorough salting called rousing was given after gutting, each grade being treated separately in a large tub before packing began. In addition, a handful of salt went in with each layer of herring in the barrel. It was back-breaking work, especially for the packers, constantly leaning over deep barrels stretching to the bottom to arrange the first important tier and working up until they had fitted in about eight hundred herrings.

Mrs Annie Finlayson:

"I think you could do about sixty to seventy in a minute. It all depends on the size of the fish, the size of the herring."

Miss Jean Bochel:

"We gutted and packed three barrels in an hour, three whole barrels in an hour. About seven or eight hundreds—when we gutted them first, but by the time they were filled up there were about a thousand herring in the barrel then. You started with one herring and then ye had one at each side of that and one in the middle. And you did it in three, three along the rest of the barrel, till it came to the middle. It was right across ye see and then ye started to go in then—it was really a work of art—but the bottom tier and the top tier, they were done very carefully, they had to be inspected."

A high standard of packing was demanded, and achieved, as everything had to be perfect for the buyers who tore herring from the tail upwards to taste them. The Russians opened barrels and tipped them up to see if the herring were all the same size. Barrels were chosen at random by the coopers for inspection. The test of a well-packed barrel was that the layers of herring remained in place even when the whole barrel was removed.

Miss Jean Bochel:

"I got away without being inspected because when I started we had a very hard foreman at the time, and oh I've been in tears many a time with him, because if it wasn't done right he would empty it out and he would say, 'You can do anything quicker doing it properly than doing it half shot.' I sure was taught the hard way but in my later years I blessed that man many a time because he saved me pounds. And in anything that you're doing it's easier and quicker to do it the right way than the wrong way.

"It had to be inspected so there was great competition among the girls. In the dinner hour we wouldn't take the hour, ye see, we'd be back quickly to our work tae get some o' this bottom tiers in before the hour to start would come—I would put in the bottom tiers ye see, whenever the hour would start the two gutters would help us to

Gutting at the farlin, c. 1920.

Nairn lassies, Lerwick, c. 1920. Note the tied fingers.

Herring Shoals

Ian Sinclair

I'm a fish gutting las-sie gutting her ring's my trade, But I'll ne-ver be weal--thy no for-tunes are made. For ten–pence a bar–rel is all we are paid, Life is hard with the her — ring shoals.

CHORUS

Oh! we'll gut and we'll clean and we'll salt them aw — ay, Fill up the bar — rels and earn a day's pay. And when the job's ov — er we'll be on our way, We'll foll — ow the her — ring shoals.

The work is gey hard and the weather is cold,
But we'll sing while we wait for that catch of pure gold.
Then the drifters sail in, what a sight to behold,
Hurrah for the herring shoals.

We gut and we salt in the sun wind and rain,
Backs almost breaking, hands stiff with pain,
But when next season comes we'll be back here again,
Along with the herring shoals.

The season is over our work is now done,
The men, with their boats and the herring have gone.
Now we've packed up our kists and we're heading for home,
Goodbye to the herring shoals.

FINAL CHORUS

For we've gutted and cleaned and we've salted away,
Filled up the barrels and earned our day's pay.
And now the job's over we'll be on our way,
We followed the herring shoals.

pack up. They would start right away while the other girls, they'd be waiting on the cooper tae come and inspect them and that held them up. So there was a row one time, this girl was mad at us for gettin' started, so the foreman took her, he says 'Come here then,' and he took her over to my barrel, he says, 'When you can do a tier like that you'll maybe be allowed to start right away too,' so that was the end of the story."

Mrs Chrissie Campbell:
"The coopers was roch and ready, ken what ah mean, they gave an oath noo and again, but ye jist took that in yer stride, ye ken, they were a' good, maist o' them was a' fine chiels ye ken."

'Filling up' was done the day following the first packing, but Mondays were often used for this work because the boats had not yet brought in fresh supplies of fish for gutting. As the salt drew moisture out of them, the herring sank down and fish from other barrels were used for filling up. The barrels, with lids on, were then laid on their sides and had bung holes drilled in them. Pickle was poured in and the barrels left for eight to ten days. After this they were turned on end and the pickle drained off, the lid removed and a second 'filling up' done if necessary. The top layer was then carefully arranged and the barrel sealed at the top. Pickle was poured in until the barrel was filled to capacity. Bungs were replaced and the barrels arranged three tiers high on their sides to await shipment. Two girls and two coopers lifted them up with the help of cleeks attached to the rims. To get the third tier into place they stood on upturned barrels. As well as helping with this heavy work, the girls were called out to bring supplies ashore when the stock boats arrived at Lerwick with salt and empty barrels.

Mrs Eveline Crockett:
"We hid tae lift barrels and dinna tell me that it didna tell on us in later life, especially if we wis haein the bairns. I mind I had my first baby, the doctor said tae me, 'You fisher quines, I dinnae like tae ging til because yer bodies are finished before ye begin.' We blamed liftin' the barrels o' herrin' on the top, a' tier abune tier. Now that wasna richt—we couldna do it."

There were no prescribed hours for gutting. When herring came in the girls worked until they were all cleared, however long this took. They were prepared for anything from the lull between catches when there was nothing to do but knit—to the big rush caused by a glut, when the work might last from 6 a.m. till 10 p.m. The obsession with earning a wage for themselves and their families did not prevent the girls from seeing the industry in a wider perspective and realising the importance of their own role within it. This is revealed in the following story of a strike in Yarmouth in the 1920s by the Scots fisher lassies who saw the Scots fleet suffering a disadvantage in relation to the English fleet because of the Scots fishermen's Sabbatarian religious principles.

Mrs Eveline Crockett:
"The English fishermen went oot on a Sunday and they gathered their harvest and delivered them on Monday which filled up oor farlins. Noo the Scotchmen didna go oot till Monday—they rested on Sunday and of course therefore oor farlins were filled and we couldna manage tae gut the twa. Nae that I have ony what ye would ca' animosity towards the English, no—but I saw it wasn't justice tae gut the Englishman's herrin' and let our Scotchman's herrin' lie tae get an affa puir

Above: A cooper inspecting the second 'filling up'. Yarmouth, c. 1924. Opposite: Eveline Reid (Crockett) dressed for camera, c. 1921.

price—gut the lot fur fish meal! So something had to be done about it and I don't like strikes by any means, but the only thing that I could see was that we had tae stop guttin' the Englishmen's fish. So twa skippers came tae me and said tae me, the only thing that ye can dae is stop guttin' them. Well, it wis nae use o' oor farlins being stopped, we had tae get the whole lot oot. So I went from yard tae yard and explained tae the girls that it wisnae oor money that kept up oor home, it was oor fishermen's money. Therefore they wasnae gettin' it, owing to this, coming in on Monday and delivering on Tuesday. Now, I took out eight hundred of us, I think. But that couldn't last because the herrin' had to be cured, it had tae be salted or they would have lost the Russian market. Therefore, there was a meeting that night, and it wis decided that half the English fleet would gang oot on a Sunday and the next half would go out the next Sunday which made matters much much better and wir fishermen did get their price and we did gut their herrin'. So the strike was only a two-day strike and it was very successful."

The English fleet were not the only ones to be conquered by Mrs Crockett's ebullient determination.

Mrs Eveline Crockett:
"I didn't mention that I had twa hours in the jail. That was a'richt, but ne'er mind, I coorted the bobby and I got tae the pictures at nicht wi' him so that was a'richt. That—ah'm nae mentioning—ah canna mention aboot that! (laughter)."

Humour also played its part in keeping the girls' spirits up during the long hours of work.

Mrs Annie Finlayson:
"There was one incident when we were workin' in Yarmouth at the farlin. There was two ladies that came along watchin' us, stood lookin' at us and we wis all guttin' very quickly. This girl, she was a character, she'd jist make anybody laugh ye know, and one o' this ladies had a soft hat wi' a great big wing, a feather at the top stickin' in it and she says, 'Eh, quines, look at her! Some gull's minus his wing the day!' This is the feather—a seagull she meant ye see. She had the whole place jist laughin'—of course they didn't know what we were laughin' at, for a good job. And you'd hear them sayin', 'Aren't they quick, aren't they quick!'."

The lasting memory of the actual physical work is one of hardship and exploitation. The girls worked as hard as they possibly could in harsh conditions to keep their earnings up, but they considered £17 to £20 a good income for a season, just about the maximum obtainable. In 1911 threepence an hour was paid for filling up. Ten years later it was fourpence, by 1929 sixpence and in 1936 Miss Jean Bochel was getting tenpence. In 1911 for gutting and packing, the three

crew members shared eightpence a barrel. In the 1920s Miss Jean Bochel and her crew were still getting only tenpence a barrel. In 1929, Jean's crew filled 1,100 barrels, earning them something like £15 each plus their filling up money, and this was considered to be a very successful season.

Miss Jean Bochel:
"No money. Tenpence, which is about four pence in today's money, between three of us for gutting and packing—well say four pence an hour. When we were filling up we got four pence an hour in Lerwick because it was warm. In Yarmouth where it was cold and frosty we got sixpence an hour. Six in the morning till half-past-eight [at night]."

Mrs Eveline Crockett:
"I wouldna go back tae guttin' again, oh no, and I wouldna put nane o' mine tae the guttin'. No. It wis a primitive wey o' workin'. I hated it, I just hated it! In fact to tell you the truth, I wouldna hae gaen tull't, if it wasna fur helpin' the fishin' industry."

The memories, however, of the companionship among the girls and their brief social hours together are recalled equally vividly.

Mrs Annie Finlayson:
"Oh, it was lovely, Gremista. Lovely place, away out tae Scotland Point. And then ye had the hills at the back and when ye wasna workin' ye went up there, sat up there wi' yer knittin' and the world was yer own. Ye hadna got a care in the world. Busy knittin' away and ye'd be singin' away, ye know and speakin' away and seein' the boats goin' out and comin' in. Mostly at the end ye know, it was bonny, it was lovely weather ye know."

Mrs Margaret Duthie:
"The boats used to go out and they played—every one would have a musical instrument and at night, when the sun would be goin' down, you know, there wasn't a finer sight tae see than all the boats sailing about and all the music going—it was just lovely!"

Miss Jean Bochel:
"We were never idle. Going along the road we would be knitting, going along the road. And of course we went to church every Sunday and the Church of Scotland had a Mission, two ladies—well usually two or three ladies used to be there, they'd have first aid and they were nurses. We got up concerts and ceilidhs of our own and some nights we'd have a dance. But one lady, she didn't think we should be dancing, it wasn't right. We says, 'What's wrong with dancing?' She says, 'There's nothing wrong with dancing, but,' she says, 'you've to go home after the dance.' (laughs) We'd a

Girls knitting outside the huts at Gremista, Shetland, c. 1910.

quarrel now and again with one another and then that would be the end of it. There was no time for moods and carrying on. Most of the courting was done during the fishing season, because when we were away from home, well the boyfriends would come up and that was when it was done. Not that it helped me any, I'm not married yet! (laughter)"

The weekend reunion with their menfolk, who amongst hundreds of others had brought in the fish which the girls so deftly handled during the past days, was the highlight of the week. There was plenty to talk about, news from home, reports on catches, prices, wedding plans. The week's hard toil was forgotten as interesting and happy talk took over, soon leading to fun and laughter from the teasing of the men. Home-made scones and pancakes, shop-bought cakes, cheese and ham were some of the delicacies provided by the girls for supper. As the evening wore on, thoughts turned to God in thankfulness for happy family relationships and the love of friends and neighbours. Speaking gave way to singing, laughter to praise, as the well-tuned voices joined together in harmonic renderings of favourite Sankey's hymns, metrical psalms, and paraphrases. For the tie which bound them together most of all, and to which they gave expression every day in honest toil and selfless devotion to each other, was their shared and constant Christian faith. When they sang, 'Will your anchor hold in the storms of life?' they never doubted that it would. Their still point was God, their 'one for the road' a psalm of praise or a hymn of hope.

Mrs Annie Finlayson:
"Oh yes, we'd oor happy times, oh yes, and if we were finished early on a Saturday then on Sunday of course we always went to church on Sunday, walked two miles into Lerwick, and then of course if the boats were in there's maybe some o' oor own friends, oor own folk, oor own men folk visited us and we'd quite a social life. And then of course we visited one hut tae the other ye know, got all the news o' home. The day the letters came ye went from one place tae see what was doin' ye know—see was there anything new at home.

"Ye all joined in [the singing]. 'Will Your Anchor Hold?', it's a great one, and 'What a Friend we have in Jesus', and another one—it was a great one that was a hymn o' mine that I liked very much too:

> 'The sands of time are sinking;
> The dawn of heaven breaks;
> The summer morn I've sighed for,
> The fair, sweet morn, awakes.
> Dark, dark hath been the midnight,
> But dayspring is at hand,
> And glory, glory dwelleth
> In Immanuel's land.'

I think we had an awful lot o' faith."

MARGARET BOCHEL

Gallipoli

"Through the narrows of the Dardanelles and across the ridges of the Gallipoli peninsula lie some of the shortest paths to a triumphant peace."
—Churchill

By the spring of 1915, the Allied armies that had marched against the Hun with such gaiety the previous August were bogged down in the trenches of France and Flanders. As casualties on the Western Front mounted, Winston Churchill conceived the scheme of using Britain's mastery of the seas to outflank Germany. When Turkey entered the war on the German side at the end of October 1914, the difficulty of maintaining contact with the Russian Empire had become greater than ever; Churchill's plan was to use sea-power to force a passage through the Turkish kyle of the Dardanelles, take Gallipoli and capture Constantinople.

Gallipoli was the long finger of land thrusting into the Aegean from the Turks' foothold in Europe. To the south stretched the heartland of the Ottoman Empire, on whose coast, just a matter of miles from the site of the coming battles, lay the plain of Troy, where Agamemnon brought his thousand ships to rescue Helen, and from whose shores Ulysses launched his epic Odyssey. The area surrounding the great sea-bridge of the Dardanelles, connecting the Mediterranean and the Black Seas, was rich in the history and legend of war.

Herodotus, Book 7, records:
"And now, as he looked and saw the whole Hellespont covered with vessels of his fleet and all the shore and every plain about Abydos as full as possible of men, Xerxes congratulated himself upon his good fortune; but after a little while he wept."

In strategic terms, the concept of the Gallipoli expedition had much to recommend it. When the straits were taken, an arms supply route would be opened to the Czar. It would also safeguard the Suez Canal, permit armed support for the Serbs, and rally other Balkan nations to the Allied cause—or at least intimidate them from joining the German. High hopes were entertained on all sides of a successful campaign, a hope reflected in the tone of King George's message to the Highland Mounted Brigade as they left England, under the command of Lord Lovat.

George V:
"I send you and your Brigade my best wishes on your departure to active service. I feel sure that the great and traditional fighting reputation of Scotsmen will be more than safe with you and that your Brigade will spare no effort in the interests of the Empire's cause to bring this war to a victorious conclusion."

Lovat's Highlanders were not the first of their people, nor the last, to fight in the Empire's cause, and most of them were Gaelic-speaking crofters, game-keepers, or estate employees on the Fraser of Lovat lands. Few knew the meaning of the word mobilisation when they were called up on the outbreak of the war, and most expected it to be a short affair culminating in the usual imperial victory.

Murdo MacLennan:
"The men that were in those days in the Scouts were outstanding. Strong men, tremendous men. I joined the Lovat Scouts in 1911, and we did drills at the Drill Hall and then we got mounted exercises on the machair. And at that time you had to provide your own horse. When the war broke out I joined the Scouts at a place called Huntingdon and then we rode from Grimsby on horseback to a place called Hunstanton in Norfolk—it took us three days, going round the Wash, through Sandringham estate, and we landed at Hunstanton, where we were until we went away to the war. The war was to be over in six months. That was the sort of conception. Everybody was anxious to get to the war—back in six months. But it was a long six months!"

In the first three months of the war alone, the Allies had lost one million casualties, and First Lord of the Admiralty Churchill's plan to open a second front at Gallipoli was widely seen as the way out of the French impasse. The plan was to land 75,000 men in April 1915 in an assault at the south on Cape Helles and at Anzac Cove, as it would soon be known, a few miles to the north. (In the event, there was to be another major invasion the following August, and the casualty rate was such that reinforcements were constantly being drafted onto the peninsula right up till the final evacuation.) The colonial troops would then seize the Mel Tepe hill, from which, so long ago, Xerxes had viewed his fleet in the Dardanelles, and command the upstream narrows across which he had built his bridge of boats for the invasion of Europe; the narrows across which Leander swam for Hero, and Lord Byron for a bet.

The plan was not, however, to survive the stunning mismanagement that would plague the expedition. For months the Turks had known that the invasion was on its way and had massively strengthened their defences. With days to go, there were no proper maps; there was no real knowledge concerning enemy positions, or water supplies, or landing facilities; even the depth of

Troops landing from the historic 'River Clyde'. Cape Helles, April 1915.

the water on the beaches which the army would soon storm was unknown. For the men sailing towards Gallipoli there was an early portent of what was to come.

Murdo MacLennan:

"We went into Alexandria in Egypt and were told to start unloading the saddlery and all the cavalry equipment and put it ashore. Well, we did this and then we loaded back webbing equipment and some of that webbing equipment must have been picked up off the battlefield because some of it was stained with blood."

Eventually, on the Greek island of Lemnos, the invasion force assembled.

Johnny Macrae:

"We stopped the ship and loaded onto small boats to get ashore. When we lowered them into the water they were all leaking, the whole blooming lot of them were all leaking—you were bailing water out the whole time. We arrived on the island and had a walk all round it. There was nothing on it but blooming sand, sand and rocks. The only tree I saw was on it, it was a fig tree, a little wee bitty fig tree, it was not much higher than a stone itself. I'd never seen one before—there was a wee dried fig on it, one dried fig on it, and I ate it."

Within days, the invaders were to meet the Turks. Unseasoned troops stormed ashore under the muzzles of the enemy guns and on one beach alone, five Victoria Crosses were to be won within a few hours of landing. With 2,000 men aboard, the *River Clyde* rammed the shore and attempted to disembark her cargo, in broad daylight. From a matter of yards the Turks shot them to pieces, many dying in the assault launches shoulder to shoulder, unable even to lift a rifle. Soon the ship's special assault-gangways were clogged with the dead and dying. Barely 200 of the 2,000 got ashore alive. An R.F.C. pilot flew over at the time and reported that in bright sunshine the sea was 'absolutely red with blood' from the beach to fifty yards offshore, whipped into a foam by the fantastic rifle, machine-gun and shrapnel fire from the enemy. But despite frightful casualties, the 30,000-strong force managed to hold by the end of that day a bridgehead at Helles and in the north at Anzac.

John Brown:

"We hung out till daylight, outside W Beach. Well, we all went up the beach, got up the top of the rise, spread out in extended order and then we got our first touch of shell fire. We were a bit scared at first, but you couldn't do anything but duck. At that time they weren't high explosive shells, they were all shrapnel and they burst thirty feet up in the air. It was a tongue of land with a mountain across it, right across the peninsula. That

An illustration of the same landing.

was the problem, you see, getting past that. It was very heavily fortified, you see."

Murdo MacLennan:

"We came under fire almost immediately after we left the liner. We went in very close and then we started crowding into these coal barges and they took us in to the beach. We came under fire almost at once—rifle fire and machine-gun fire. Of course the barges grounded when they were quite a bit out from the beach and it was a case of jumping over the side. We lost quite a lot of men one way and another—in some places there was barbed wire in the sea and some of the guys were getting mixed up in it. But anyway, we got ashore. That was near Chocolate Hill—the name was given to the place because it was all churned up with shells and trenches, and it looked like the colour of chocolate. It had been cultivated in some sort of way before we landed there and there were water melons and tomatoes growing about the place, but they didn't last long. Some of the guys lost their lives going out after water melons between the two lines."

Within a fortnight it was clear that the invasion had lost any impetus it might once have had. There were already 25,000 casualties, all the reserves and most of the shells had gone, and the two landings still held just five square miles of the peninsula. The guns of the artillery were rationed to two shells a day, and the King's 'poor bloody infantry' settled in on their beachheads, eye to eye with 'Johnny Turk'.

John Brown:

"They were anything from 25 to 200 yards away. You see, between a front-line and a support trench, you have a communication trench. So when we took one of their front-line trenches, you worked your way along the communication trench and built a barricade, and threw bombs over it at them. They were home-made bombs at the time, pound jam tins filled with bits of shrapnel, gelignite and a fuse—that gave you five seconds. Sometimes they would throw one over and we would pick it up and throw it back again before it got time to explode—we were just taking a chance. There was shells coming in all the time. You were a wee bit better in the firing line than the supports. In the firing line, see, you didn't get the shells so bad, we were so close to their own men they were afraid they would hit them instead of us.

"There was one fellow, they called him Bun Craig, jolly type o' fellow, he came round the corner o' the traverse—he'd a hole in his cheek, right through. He must have had his mouth open but a bullet had gone right through one cheek, out the other. And he says, 'Here, Jock, look what the so 'n' so's have done tae ma face!' And he was splutter, spluttering blood all over the place, ye see. Well, anyway, we'd tae tie him up, and he wanted

A shell from the Turkish gun 'Asiatic Annie' bursts in the sea near Cape Helles. The men shelter under the cliff.

Banks of the Bosphorus

March

Pipe Major J. Robertson

John Brown, a survivor. c. 1916.

a smoke. Here he found that he couldn't smoke—kept blowin' the smoke out through the hole in his cheek! You heard him swearing—we had tae hold his cheek tae let him get a smoke!"

Johnny Macrae:
"Oh, they were just ordinary trenches, you know, with a firing step. You had to watch yourself there, you know, there was sniping all the time, you know, day and night."

Murdo MacLennan:
"I was a sniper for a while myself and it's not a very nice job. There was a big tree in front of us, and we fixed steel plates in it. You went out there before daylight and you were there till night, overlooking the Turkish trenches. Once they started to shell this tree with high explosives and they nearly blew it out of the ground. But they never hit the fellow that was in it, no—but he was chittering with fright

for about a week after he got out of it that night. A fleet of destroyers used to come in during the day and fire away at the Turks. When the *Queen Elizabeth* used to fire her sixteen-inch guns, while the flames lasted from the muzzle of the gun, you could actually see the shadow of the shell leaving it.

"There was a lot of poor work with our own guns—some of their shells falling among us, you know. Before you went in you were frightened. But after you got mucked in, the fear sort of left you. Sometimes conditions were so bad you didn't care whether you were shot or not. When the whistle blew, you just went over the top and ran like steam, through the wire and into the other fellow's trench and went at it, hand to hand. Rifle and bayonet, yes. You fired from the hip, you know, you were right in among them."

By June, the plague of flies that infested the place were growing fat and bloated on blood. Conditions became worse than ever, and men broke teeth trying to eat the army ration biscuits upon which they largely existed.

Murdo MacLennan:
"Bully beef and hard biscuits—that was it. Sometimes you had to pound them up with an entrenching tool before you could even look at them."

Making bombs from empty jam tins.

Anzac Cove, troopships landing.

Johnny Macrae:

"The food that was on the peninsula was just a lot of bully beef and biscuits, hard biscuits, and tea. But sugar was scarce, and so was milk. And water was scarce as well."

Poor food and grossly insanitary conditions led to massive losses through disease and sickness.

Murdo MacLennan:

"One of the worst features of the peninsula was disease—dysentry, malaria, trench fever. Trench fever was where men were overloaded with lice, and sores got to be all over them. Dysentry was deadly. In five days you would see a stalwart man reduced to a wretch, they just laid down and didn't even bother going to the rear. It was terrible, and I think the dysentry was due to the fact that the dead weren't properly buried. The ground was hard and they weren't buried deep enough and when heavy rain came you could see a man lying in his grave, you could see his face and his hands. We got our water out of wells that were dug in the cemetery and I think that had a lot to do with it. We lost a tremendous lot of men with the dysentry."

John Brown:

"And then my hands were all one mass of septic sores. They're still shiny to this day. You got septic sores with your hands rubbing against the side of the trenches. We used to carry a bag of bandages and a wee bottle of carbolic acid, you put a drop or two in some water and bathed the sores. And all the time a lot of us were rotten with dysentry. I managed to dodge it. But I took jaundice, yellow jaundice. But it didn't make any difference, they were so short of men you just had to fight on."

Murdo MacLennan:

"Ships were being sunk on the way out and we were short of everything and there wasn't much coming ashore in the way of medical supplies. The men were sometimes tearing their underclothes to wrap round their wounds."

By August the Allies were ready to attempt another offensive, centred on Anzac and Suvla Bay to the north of it. At Suvla, 25,000 men were to storm ashore and across the bed of the dried-up Salt Lake. Almost 40,000 fresh reinforcements were to break out from the Anzac bridgehead, and put an end to the Turks. Given proper leadership, they would have, but the chain of command broke down completely. At Suvla, the attackers spent

Soldiers crossing the Salt Lake at Suvla, August 1915.

the whole day wandering on the plain, held back by just 1,500 Turks without a machine-gun among them. Not till dusk did they advance and take Chocolate Hill, after a 24-hour delay in which the Turks were rushing reinforcements to the front. At Anzac the charge took place in broad daylight across a front just 200 yards wide—in the first few days alone, 4,000 men died, and seven Victoria Crosses were awarded. At Sari Bair, the commanders considered sending in the Australian Light Horse in a cavalry charge—but they were finally dismounted and charged Battleship Hill. Half of their 1,200 men were dead in minutes. Not till the end of August did the battle come to an end and 45,000 Allied soldiers were casualties in those weeks alone.

John Brown:

"Now we went over the top after three or four hours bombardment in the morning. We were told to take three lines of trenches. We cleared the first and we cleared the second and we went into the third and the third was a dummy, it was only a foot deep. We got an awful cutting up there, we lost about 400 men in that stunt. You had to chase them out with the bayonet, you see, you had to go over and chase them out. It was just hell, I don't like to describe it, you just dived in hoping that he would clear off! After a trench was taken it was just dead

all over the place, full up of dead, and we had to live among them, until we could dig another trench alongside and fill them in, you know, in the old trench. Sometimes the trench had so many dead in it, you didn't know where to put them. We sometimes had to bury our own dead in the sides of the communication trench—you just dug a hole down from the top, put it in, and one or two sandbags on top. But them that were killed in between the lines, they lay there all the time. And after a stunt the place was living with maggots, crawling with maggots, you see. It was absolutely one desperate stench, but if it was a while since the action, if it was quiet for a bit, the smell died down and wasn't so bad, if the wind wasn't in the wrong direction."

Many of the soldiers in the Gallipoli invasion forces were not native-born Englishmen. Scottish regiments like the Highland Light Infantry and the King's Own Scottish Borderers saw action on the peninsula, as did Welsh and Irish soldiers, Sikhs from India, and the incomparable Anzacs, insubordinate and brave in equally heroic proportions.

Murdo MacLennan:

"They were very fine chaps. Reckless to a

Australians freezing by their dugouts, November 1915.

degree, you know, they were mostly the Light Horse. I came across a lot of them and they were quite the finest set of men I have ever seen. Oh yes, great physique and good appearance. Aye, wonderful men."

Angus MacVarish:
  "They were great friends of the Scottish soldiers, but they didn't like the English so much at all."

Murdo MacLennan:
  "The man in the next bay to me was a Gurkha and I got very pally with him. I gave him a wrist watch that wasn't going but he didn't mind that. He said, 'You are my blood brother', and this is the mark he put on my hand with his kukri [Gurkha knife]—it'll never go away. It's been there sixty-six years now. Whatever he put in it, I don't know. He used to give me chapatties and that sort of thing, and, oh, they liked their rum ration, the Gurkhas. They were very fond of the rum. When the ration would come round, they would say, rum tonight, charge tomorrow! You often got an issue of rum, you know, before you went in for an attack, whether it was to boost your morale or not I don't know."

  Not all of the incidents on the peninsula were tragic, and the soldiers thought up ingenious ways to keep their spirits up.

John Brown:
  "Once we made a fiddle, a Japanese fiddle, just a box with a handle, very crude, but we managed to get a tune out of it. We put a field telephone wire on it for a string and hair from a mule's tail. We just used to boil the hair to get the grease out of it and we managed to get it to play, just the usual Scottish tunes, you know."

Murdo MacLennan:
  "On one occasion on the front-line, Gallipoli, the officers thought, well, we'll get our pipe band together and we'll play a selection (laughing)—we were only about 75 yards away from the Turks at the time. So they got a hold of Pipe Major Donald Macmillan and got that band gathered together and they set up their pipes. Well, boy! did we pay for it! There was grass, long white grass in front of the trenches and they set the grass on fire with shell fire and oh it was terrific, terrific! The Colonel said, 'Well, this is a good idea for making the Turks waste a lot of ammunition!' (laughter)."

  It was becoming increasingly clear to the General Staff that the campaign was a failure, and as autumn set in with the prospect of severe weather in the near future, even the once-high morale of the army began to drain away. Hugh Cameron had been priest in Castlebay, Barra, and at the age of forty had volunteered as chaplain to the Catholic soldiers with

Father Hugh Cameron, Chaplain to the Lovat Scouts at Suvla.

the Highland Mounted Brigade at Gallipoli. The entries in his private diary reflect the falling spirits of the soldiers, and the endless round of life on the peninsula—shelling, sniping, stand-to's, listening posts in no-man's-land, scouting, disease, burial parties, and growing hopelessness.

Father Cameron:
"Mass this morning at six-thirty. What a figure I must have cut—muddy slacks, tunic covered with dirt, unshaven. Luckily the guns were quiet, but a few bullets were coming over the parapet and whistling over my head. The strain on my back and through stooping was awful. All the men were at Holy Communion. One of the Mallaig boys was shot while on sentry—lucky boy, just a scalp wound. Yesterday we were heavily shelled. Major Grant was badly wounded last night while spying. One of the Moidart boys was killed, a bullet through the head while standing on the firing bank. Terrible shelling this morning."

By November the weather was worse than ever, but the generals and politicians still argued about evacuation. The British guns were down to a ration of two shells a day each, and winter clothing had still not arrived. Many units were at half-strength, and Staff estimates of an evacuation-casualty rate were around 40 per cent or 40,000 men. As the weather worsened

day by day, the prospect grew of the whole army being cut to ribbons on storm-lashed evacuation beaches. On the 27th of November, the worst weather in forty years hit the Gallipoli peninsula.

Willie Fraser:
"That night there was thunder and lightning and the Turks—I think they thought they were going to wallop us off Suvla Bay—they let a dam go way up in the hills, down through Chocolate Hill, and the rivers got flooded. All our trenches were flooded to the top. We couldn't get a rifle to fire in the muck—and then the frost set in and in the morning an awful lot had frostbite."

Murdo MacLennan:
"Things were so bad we had to get everything we could lay our hands on to light a fire. It gives you an idea of how bad things were when we weren't even firing at each other. For two nights we could see each other quite plain round the fires."

The rain lasted for a full twenty-four hours, and then the wind veered to the north, increased to hurricane force, and brought snow—the first snow the Anzacs had ever seen. Sentries froze to death at their posts and when the storm subsided, the army had lost a tenth of its strength. Two hundred men were drowned, 5,000 disabled with frostbite, and another 5,000 also hospitalised. Evacuation fever gripped the increasingly bitter army.

Father Cameron:
"Rumours of evacuation. The sooner the better. None of us will be sorry to leave this damned hole of a graveyard where so many brave men have fallen in vain. We are all having visions of Egypt, where they will send us next. This is for my own use and I can put down my own thoughts for they are the thoughts of all of us. From start to finish Gallipoli has been a most abominably managed business. Had the fine material available been properly handled we should long ago have been in Stamboul instead of holding three miles of flat dominated on three sides by the Turks. We were up on those heights more than once and bad leadership in high places lost them to us. That is what makes the temper of the army so bitter. Our Brigade are to fight our way out. I shall send this diary by one of those who go before me in the hope that it may eventually reach home if I do not. Oh Lord, give me the grace to do my duty like a man."

The rumours were correct—the army was to be evacuated, whatever the casualty rate. The retreat in fact was the only success of the whole campaign. With incredible luck, the army got off Gallipoli with scarcely a casualty—its secret phased withdrawal worked to perfection. The weather held just long enough for the army to get away.

Farewell to Cape Helles

Retreat

Pipe Major William Ferguson

First time

Second time

John Brown:

"I volunteered to stay in the front-line till the end but we didn't know everyone had gone till the afternoon, when one of our fellows nipped back to the support to get some water and when he came back he says, 'Here, fellows, there's not a bugger in the supports!' So we had the wind up then, good and proper, in case Johnny Turk put in an attack. If he had, I don't know what we'd have done. There was just twenty of us, instead of two or three thousand. When it got dark it was just absolutely awful, you know. Time, och it was like years, like

Lord Kitchener at Gallipoli. Kitchener decided that evacuation was inevitable.

waiting for years, you see. I never put in such a time in my life, waiting, waiting, absolutely sick with anxiety.

"Well, we were withdrawing from all points, and as we went down there was more and more of us till there was quite a wee battalion of us. When we got down onto the beach one of the brasshats met us, and he was nearly crying with relief to see us arriving there. He didn't expect to see us make it, you see. But we got to the beach at last, and onto a barge and out to a destroyer. We were so beat, so fatigued, we could hardly climb up, but we were hauled up and we just threw ourselves down and I remember one of the sailors looking at us, and he says—'Oh, poor buggers'."

Willie Fraser:

"So we got to the beach in the dark and we got through the wire and then we knew we were safe because the barges were waiting. And all of a sudden, as we were going off, we heard a jangling on the barbed wire. There was this mule that had been left behind, and he came charging down, you know, and into the wire, and that's the last I remember seeing of Suvla Bay—a mule dangling on the barbed wire about thirty yards from the beach."

In the nine months of the Gallipoli campaign, the Allies deployed half a million soldiers, and half of them became casualties. Turkish losses probably were higher. The assessment of those who remember the peninsula sixty-six years after leaving it is still tinged with some bitterness about a campaign to whose fighting soldiers no special medal was ever awarded.

John Brown, 1981, fashioning a fiddle. He made his first instrument on Gallipoli.

Murdo MacLennan:

"Well, there was a shortage of everything—medicine, bandages, ammunition for guns and rifles, food, water. For a while we just got a pint of water a day for everything."

John Brown:

"The officers, we hadn't any feeling against the officers, they were in it the same as us. But the high-ups, we didn't think so much of them, we didn't think we were getting a very fair do from them. I never felt I would get off Gallipoli, never thought it was possible. If we didn't get killed, we would die of starvation or disease, you understand. That's what we feel about Churchill. He was detested, the man was always detested for that—by those who knew the place. It's a place you hardly hear mentioned, though you hear plenty about the rest of the war. I believe it was squashed, the whole thing was squashed. I had a year in France but it wasn't anything like the horrors of Gallipoli."

Murdo MacLennan:

"Oh, the country was bled white, bled white. Where I come from, there were seven young men killed, out of a total population of a hundred. It was the same all over the Highlands. There was a lot of mismanagement. You were put in to attack in broad daylight, what they called stunts. 'We'll try a stunt,' they'd say, and they'd put in a battalion or thereabouts and they would be massacred."

Due to the numbers involved, the tragedy of Gallipoli has passed into the folklore of Scotland's working people. But bitterness is not the prerogative of the ordinary soldiers who saw service there. Lord Lovat, invalided out of the peninsula with dysentry, wrote from hospital to his wife about the campaign, with a damning indictment of the whole Gallipoli adventure.

Lord Lovat:

"It is more than clear that Winston alone was the inspiration of this tragedy. The Gallipoli expedition properly carried out would have been brilliant; great strategic possibilities and with combined action (Army and Navy) very little risk; carried out piecemeal, sailors first, driblets of soldiers second, more driblets of soldiers third, starvation of guns fourth, failure to observe Balkan trouble fifth, plus final debacle on arrival of guns and supplies through Serbia, it was disaster. It will be up to date and probably to all eternity as sordid and miserable a chapter of amateur enterprise as ever was written in our history."

IAIN FRASER GRIGOR

The Pearl Fishers

THE PEARL FISHER

Where the Tay, the Earn and the Isla flow
Threadin wi siller the plaid o' the strath
Kneedeep in river shallows gaes the pearl fisher,
Wi sunbaked, wind-hardened face bent on the water.
Keen-eyed, he peers intae the shingle bed,
For the fabled shell, the yin he dreams o'
The secret, hidden, unexpectit yin tae make his fortune.

For that he tholes the cauld and bous his back
For oors and days, aften wi nae reward.
He never heeds the warld aroon
Wha's sichts and soonds a' melt awa.

His lassie's een an breists, his bairnies' lachter,
Firelicht, gowd o hairst,
Birdsang wi the day dawning,
The fiddlers' rant wi the feet dirlin;
His faither deid, his hame brunt doon,
His siller tane or his dochter hured,
It a' means nowt tae him, noo doif an blin
As if by warlock cantrip tane,
Tae a' but the socht for prize:
The ae perfect and priceless pearl.

—Sheila Douglas

'The ae perfect and priceless pearl' has been 'socht for' in the rivers of Scotland from before Roman times. It is said that pearls were one of the prizes sought by the Phoenicians when they landed in Britain. At that time most of Britain's rivers were the habitat of the river mussel which produced the pearls but today Scotland is one of the few places left in Europe with some of its rivers unpolluted. Over the last 300 years there are records of the great quality and quantity of Scottish pearls and we are fortunate today that the river mussel can still survive in so many rivers of the Highlands and the north-east free from the pollution of industry.

The most common pearls are found in oysters in Oriental seas and these pure white, round, precious jewels are most people's image of what a pearl looks like. The river pearls can vary enormously in quality but they also vary in colour and lustre which can make them more interesting than the Oriental variety.

The traditional belief, the world over, was that the pearl was formed from a grain of sand which irritated the oyster or the mussel. This belief is not far from the truth but it is now more certain that the pearls are formed by a parasite which enters the shell. An irritation sets in which the mussel isolates and gradually covers with layer upon layer of mother of pearl. This process can take many years and it is now

Opposite: A pearl fisher, Bill Abernethy.

evident that many of the mussels can be up to 150 years old. The river mussel can only survive in clean, fresh water and this is why so many of the fast flowing rivers of the Scottish Highlands are so perfect a habitat.

In the *Book of the Pearl*, published in 1908, there is a record from as early as 1560 when 'large, handsome pearls' were sent from Scotland to Antwerp. In 1620 a great pearl was found in the Kellie burn in Aberdeenshire; this was carried to King James by the provost of Aberdeen, who was rewarded with 'twelve to fourteen chalder of victuals about Dunfermline and the Customs of Merchants goods in Aberdeen during his life'. There are also accounts of how between 1761 and 1764 £10,000 worth of pearls were sent to London and sold from ten shillings to one pound six shillings per ounce. In 1861 a German merchant travelled through the districts of the Tay, Doon and Don and interested the local people in gathering pearl mussels. 1862 was a particularly good year, owing to the dryness of the season and in the low water unusually large quantities of pearls were found. The *Book of the Pearl* brings its history up to the turn of the present century with accounts of pearls bought by Empress Eugenie and Queen Victoria herself.

Until recent years this long tradition of pearl fishing was continued almost exclusively by members of the travelling people who, in between seasonal farm work in the summer, camped by the rivers and searched for pearls.

Peter McMillan:
"It was fifty years ago that I started with my father, we all pearlfished then, my uncles and brothers and cousins. I think the whole family used to go up to the Spey to pearl fish, all the season, from April to September, and we got a lot of good pearls then, big ones, you know, and some small stuff and that. I've seen dozens of us fishing together, not only my family but other families too in the travelling family class, we always fished. We used to meet up there every year and we all fished in the Spey, and the Tay, the river Morrison, the Conan, we fished all these rivers in our younger days.

"But it was a hard life then for us youngsters, it was very hard. Travelling from one place to another, up and down the river, way over to Blairgowrie, down the Tay and away up to Glen Lyon—horse and cart then, or a caravan. We all went under canvas then and we camped there all summer, you know, pearl fishing all the time, as long as the river was fishable, like."

The river mussel is usually found in the bed of the river and very often almost completely hidden from view.

Pearling from a boat.

Bill Abernethy:

"The equipment is simple, all you need is a forked stick and a glass-bottomed bucket to cut off the ripple of the water. You can wade to quite deep water, maybe five or six feet, but if it's any deeper than that, you need a boat. You see the bottom of the river with your glass and you pick up the shells, it's just as simple as that. But there's other little wrinkles that you've got to know—where the pearls are and things like that. There's certain weeds that grow and certain types of gravel and all that comes into consideration, the flow of the water and things like that. There's quite a few things that you've got to know to be successful at it."

Betsy Whyte:

"My father and most travellers made their own boats for pearl fishing. They used to get wood from a sawmill or something, wide planks. They weren't deep these boats and they were shaped a bit like, you've seen a snow plough at the front, well, they used to bend their wood over like that at the front, and the back was straight. It was completely flat on the bottom and maybe just about twenty inches deep, just shallow boats. They put planks along the straight back and these planks would act as a seat if you were sitting in the boat and when you were pearl fishing you lay on your belly on top of these planks with your head over the side of the boat. I used to watch them sitting making them, getting the wood and getting it fixed together and then you've got tar, I'm sure it was tar you put on them to make them waterproof. And a lot of the travellers did the same. They were very light, you could carry them on your shoulders when you were shifting about, if the water was too shallow, you could just put it up on your head and walk with it,

it was that light. And yet they were strong, 'cause sometimes if the water was deep enough you were moving down the river, he'd get us all into the boat and it was great, we used to scream, laugh and carry on and he says, 'If the baillies haven't seen me, they're sure to have heard me.' Because they chased us about that much up the river, you ken. And all the travellers' boats were built like that. Just simple things but they worked.

"From a very early age, we got to recognise the pearl shells, a lot of folk call them mussels but I never connected them with a mussel. They're a bit like a mussel but much longer and flatter. You can get them about ten, twelve inches long, very big and sometimes they get a bit damaged. Did you ever see an auld burned boot? Well, you get shells much the shape of that and almost as big and these were the ones we loved to get, they were almost sure of a pearl but sometimes they were disappointing too because the pearl might turn out to be brown or blae coloured and these were valueless. Very rarely you got tiny seeds of black pearls but in all those years of fishing my father never got a decent sized black pearl. They're very rare but they are there, but he never happened to get one. There were lots of different shapes and sizes of pearls and you often got things just like a pearl but it was just a big cluster sticking to the shell and this was very disappointing. These were valueless although they were nice to look at. Then you would often get two or more pearls in a shell or sometimes a cluster of tiny seed pearls and you could get something for them, for setting in rings and brooches. Then there were brown pearls and they were valueless. But sometimes you could get a lovely clear pearl and a fine size, maybe the size of a round pea, and take it home and by the time you

Travellers' camp.

got home with it, it had turned blae. Pearls did this with some people and with other people they would keep their purity. I've seen my father saying to a man that had got this big blae pearl, 'What are you doing with it?' 'Aw,' he would say, 'I'm just going to throw it away, it's no use.' He says, 'Give it to me.' So he got it, a good size of pearl, about pea size. He took it home and says, 'Maggie, put that pearl in your bosom for two or three days,' and its purity came back. You know pearls will do that. There are certain people that they will not keep their true colours with. They change. My mother was one of these people that they would keep their true colour with. My father didn't keep the money to himself, he wouldn't do that. He maybe felt like it but the travelling folk believe that if they do anything like that, they'll get paid back double for it so he shared the money with the man that had found the pearl and he says, 'Don't tell me you got that for thon pearl.' He says, 'I did.' He wouldn't believe him, he says, 'I cannae believe you.' 'Well,' my father says, 'that pearl was as pure as anything when Maggie had it for a few days.' So he would hardly go pearl fishing without my mother being there. She was just one of these kind of folk that was lucky at opening shells and that pearls kept their colour with."

The pearl fishers lived and worked by the rivers, their popularity varying according to the attitudes of the local landowners and their estate workers.

Betsy Whyte:

"We used to get chased a lot off the river but it wasn't because of taking pearls, it was always because they thought you were maybe poaching for salmon. Well travellers, they wouldn't care less about salmon because they would prefer trout, you ken. And anyway they had a sort of thing with the landowners, the gentry, as we called them, because the gentry would often stand and speak to traveller folk and ask them questions about what they were doing and they understood us much better than anybody else and they tolerated us on their grounds. They would give you a piece of ground and you could live there and they knew that they could trust us not to touch the salmon and they would ask for a pearl but they always paid for the pearls. Sometimes my father would go and give the lady of the house a pearl, he says, 'I'll give you this pearl if you'll give me a permit to fish this part of the river,' the part that they owned and they rarely refused. But that didn't keep the water bailiffs from chasing you off and breaking the boat. My father used to take great pains to hide his boat when he was going home at night because although they were very light, you didn't fancy carrying them home every night along the banks of a river, so he used to hide them in . . . grass or undergrowth—a certain way to try and hide them from the water baillies or they would chase you. I've seen it come into fights between travellers and water baillies but only if the traveller had a permit. If he didn't have a permit, he would just go quietly off the water and that was it. But if he'd got a permit from the landowner he'd just keep fishing away and ignore the bailiffs, you ken, and hae them screaming and cursing across the river, and he'd just fish away and never let on and then after they'd brought the police, they would take out their permit and say 'I've a permit to fish here from Lady So an' So', you ken, whoever it was. There's quite a lot of big estates in Perthshire, landowners, and most of them were very familiar with the travellers. If a traveller was in difficulty or trouble with the police or with fishing in the rivers, these folk, they understood right away what the travellers would do and what they wouldn't do. And what they could trust them with and what they couldn't trust them with, that sort of way. So they had what they called 'their own travellers' come here every year and I've often seen ladies in Perthshire, when an old traveller passed away, paying for the burial and everything. If there was an old woman or an old man left on their own, they would never say to them 'You'd be better going into a home or something', they understood them better than that."

For most people in the past pearlfishing was a seasonal job and for many it still is. But Bill Abernethy has made pearlfishing a full-time occupation and fishes practically all the year round, travelling all over Scotland.

Bill Abernethy:

"I just like it because it's a good job, you can go where you want and travel the country and you meet a lot of people at the rivers. There's no any hustle at the job, you've no set times from nine o'clock here or six o'clock there and all this sort of thing. You can please yourself, there's no any pressures put on you, like say you were an office worker or some job like that where you had responsibility, but at the pearl fishing there was never any push.

"My father and his brothers were at the pearl fishing at the beginning of this century and back as far as 1890. My father and his uncle started pearling here in Scotland, but at that time there were more pearl fishers than now, for a various number of reasons. At that time there wasn't the same pollution in the rivers, they were more or less free, and there were no cultured or artificial pearls or anything. All the pearls that were on the market were natural pearls, they were either freshwater pearls or pearls from the sea, and the prices were quite high according to the value of money for other jobs. A good pearl, say maybe in 1910, you would get £60 for it. Now that's near a year's wages for an ordinary man working."

The largest pearl that we know of today found in a Scottish river was found by Bill Abernethy in 1967. Today it is on show at Cairncross' jewellery shop in Perth.

Alistair Cairncross:

"The Abernethy pearl is so perfect that when we saw it first of all we immediately thought of creating the most marvellous pendant with it and the lilac tint in the pearl demanded a very special colour of diamonds to go with it. However, when we thought about it afterwards we decided that it was so lovely that it would be a crime to drill it to create a mount for it. We therefore decided just to put it on show so that the rest of the world can have a look at it whenever they feel so inclined and we have a special case in the shop in which the Abernethy pearl sits in majesty."

Bill Abernethy, who found the pearl, describes how he found it.

"Sometimes the flood covers beds of them [mussels] with leaves. It was like that on the Tay, you know, where I got the Abernethy pearl, the pearl, the big pearl. I'd fished it the year before and there hadn't been any shell but in a big back wash there had been a lot of leaves in the winter floods that had been washed down. The next year when I went, another flood had shifted them and here was a bed of shells looking up from the sand. I started digging them and then I dug this shell, it was just about that size [demonstrates] but it was about that

Travellers camp by the river.

breadth when I put the stick in you know, it would hardly go in, it was that wide and I knew when I dug it, I said, this is a good shell, because the shell with the good pearls, there's usually a bit of a twist on it. When I dug it I put it in a corner of the boat and when I came to cut the shells I had this one at one side and I knew there was a good pearl in it but what I didn't know was that it was twice the size of what it was supposed to be, you see, it was a freak of nature. It was just like a duck's egg sitting in it. You know, when I opened the shell it was just a huge bump covered in the meat and the only thing that I was worried about was, I knew it was round, I thought there might have been some mark or something on it. The pearls are encased in the meat, they're not attached to the shell, they're encased in the meat and when I squeezed it out of the meat there wasn't a mark on it. I carry a bottle, you know, for putting the pearls in, it was that big that I couldn't get it in the neck of the bottle and so I wrapped it in a docken leaf and put it in my pocket. That's how it came to light."

There are many stories about the largest, most perfect pearls that people have found.

Betsy Whyte:
"I remember one pearl that my father got and it was very big, much bigger than the average pearl, almost marble sized, a small marble. By seven or eight o'clock, they all went home together and this uncle of mine, when he was coming past, my mother said, 'Look.' 'Any luck,' he says, 'I never got a thing,' and she says 'Look' and he says 'Ach, a blowed bead,' and he just hit her hand underneath, you ken, and sent it right over among a heap of stones at the riverside, ken they wee chuckie stones at the side of the river. My father jumped after it, you ken, he'd been packing up his things and hiding his boat and when my uncle saw them desperately looking he says, 'It must have been a pearl right enough.' So in the end they hunted for hours before they found it, but they did get it. And my uncle says, 'Well, I just couldn't believe a pearl that size,' and my father got a good price for it in Perth."

The pearls found in Scottish rivers have a great variety of colour and shape and this is now an important part of their appeal.

Neil McCormick:
"You get some beautiful pearls, different colours, different shapes, different sizes. You can get them barrel shaped, pear shaped, button, like flat on the bottom and round on the top, that's button; round ones are the hardest to find, it's usually buttons or peardrops or all different, you can even get them like a corkscrew, you know. They're unique, there's no two the same, hardly any two look the same."

Examining mussels for pearls.

Bill Abernethy:
"You get them all colours, you can get them pink, mauve, purple, white, creamy coloured, salmon pink, all the different colours of the rainbow. The sea pearls, you know, they're more or less all one colour. One pearl's the same as the next, but a Scotch pearl, you can get a brooch made up or a necklace and every pearl's different, they're individual, and that seems to appeal to people as well, it makes them look more, what should I say, natural because they blend in with, more or less, the colours of the country."

Today there is only one jeweller in Scotland who buys river pearls. Alistair Cairncross in Perth creates settings and designs for the pearls found in this country. His is a family business which has dealt with pearls since 1869.

Alistair Cairncross:
"The pearls we feel are completely individual, the beauty of the pearl, the Scottish pearl in comparison with an oriental, or cultured pearl for that matter, is that they have a very very subtle quiet lustre, they're not as brilliant as an oriental, but their colouring is very much more subtle and there's a hint of the misty hills in the background in them. They, being different, require, we think, a different form of presentation and over the years

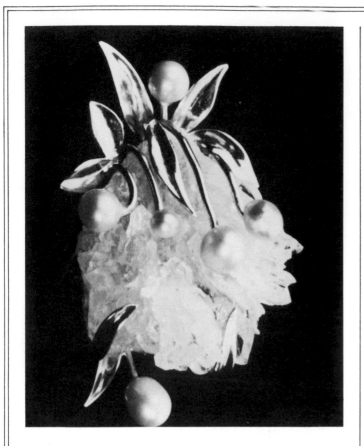

Pearls and rose quartz.

we have developed a series of designs which not only show off the pearls in their own individual way but are indicative of the atmosphere of the background in which the pearl was found. For instance, rhododendrons and rowans, a lot of the berries—blaeberries, crowberries, cranberries; this allows us to create a slightly different character to each mount.

"The supply of the pearls is rather restricted with the result that we have to try to use every pearl which has any beauty or lustre at all. Having asymmetrical designs, we're not restricted to trying to match sizes of pearls and they don't have to be round so that we can make the most use of the pearls that are available. The other type of pearl which gives us a certain amount of pleasure in using is the slightly Baroque looking pearl which might have what we term a bad end, in other words, the nacre of the pearl hasn't covered the whole pearl and it's a nice little puzzle how to use this to the best advantage so that the bad end is hidden in the mount and yet the pearl itself is happily proportioned in the design so that the whole thing looks perfectly natural and as though nature had meant it to be that way."

Bill Abernethy:

"Way back in my father's time there were jewellers all over Scotland bought pearls. There was a large number of pearl fishers and a large amount of pearls available. Tourists could buy a pearl say even in Coupar Angus here or Blairgowrie or small village jewellers. All the jewellers had a few Scotch pearls for sale. At that time there was umpteen nomadic pearl fishers going about, if they hadn't the time or the inclination maybe to go to Edinburgh or up to Aberdeen or Perth, that's where they got a bigger price for them, they would just sell them to the local jeweller. In fact there was one of the travelling crowd that goes about, he got a big pearl in the Earn, just below Crieff it was, and he went into this baker's shop and he tried to sell the pearl to the baker and the baker says 'I'll take the pearl, and anytime that you want bread,' he says, 'you can come in here and you'll get it free, if you'll gie me the pearl.' And the deal was made there and then and he had more or less a lifetime's supply of bread for this pearl. That's how the baker worked him, but I think the baker got quite a good price for that pearl because it was really a fine stone, you know; but that's how he done the deal!

"There was one particular pearl that was got in the South Esk, I think it was about 1906 by a nomadic pearl fisher by the name of 'Cove Pitcaithlie' and he travelled about all over Scotland. There was, like, several hundred pearl fishers at that time going all over the country and they just called him Cove. He got this pearl and it was a pink ball that he got, up in the South Esk just above

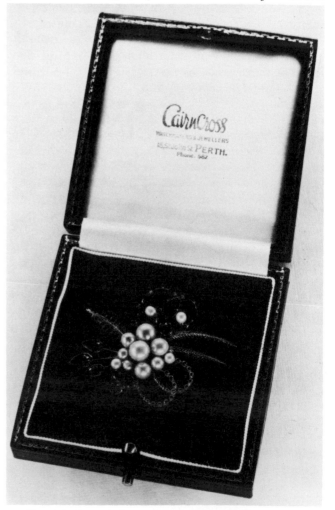

Scottish river pearls set for Her Majesty the Queen.

Brechin, and it was thirty-seven-and-a-quarter grains. It was a lovely pearl and he went into the local jeweller up in Brechin and the local jeweller offered him £20 for it. But the Cove Pitcaithlie knew that it was worth more than that and the jeweller wouldn't give him any more. Anyway it seems to have transpired that the jeweller made out that the Cove had come by the pearl other than fishing it and as he was coming out of Brechin to go down to Edinburgh to sell the pearl there were two policemen coming, legging after him and they shouted to him. But the Cove, he surmised that there was something up and he put the pearl in the cup of his clay pipe, you see, and covered it up with the tobacco and they came up to him and they asked him about this pearl and he said he didn't know anything about a pearl. But they arrested him. They said, 'You've been in a jeweller with a pearl and he's offered you £20 for it.' But they had to let him go because they couldn't find the pearl on him but he had the pearl in his clay pipe and he left Brechin then when they let him go and he had to walk to Edinburgh because he hadn't any money. He got £100 for that pearl and it was worth more even than that, but he took the £100—a hundred gold sovereigns he got for it. That pearl was sold to an Austrian count but where it went after that, they didn't know. But that one came off the South Esk, it was thirty-seven-and-a-quarter grains because my father asked the jeweller that bought it in Edinburgh because Cove Pitcaithlie, he stayed with my grandmother here in Coupar Angus and he was on about this great pearl he had. He had all thir gold sovereigns, and when they went through to Edinburgh they asked the jeweller, 'Oh aye,' he says, 'we bought that pearl, it was thirty-seven-and-a-quarter grains right enough.' They thought that the Cove was exaggerating a bit because he tended to exaggerate, but this was genuine, you know, a genuine find."

Although pure white pearls are sought after, the great prize was to find a black pearl.

Betsy Whyte:
"For years they were all hunting for a black pearl; they said they'd get a fabulous price if they could get a black pearl but I've never heard of anyone getting one except seeds, tiny seeds which weren't much good.

"You know, if you burn a pearl it'll turn black but as soon as it's handled a bit it just crumbles away. But there was this lady and she was dying for a black pearl and I think the temptation must have been too much so this woman burned these pearls and sold them to the lady. Two, they were black and shiny when she sold them. Later some of them went back to the lady's house and she said, 'You know, I don't know what's happened to these pearls, I put them away safely in the drawer but I could never find them. I questioned everybody in

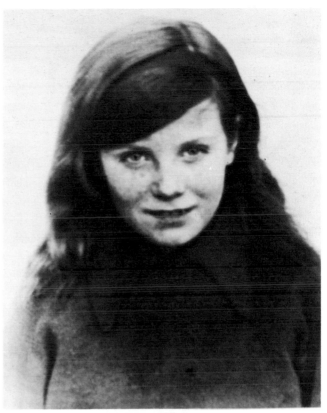

Betsy Whyte.

the house and they were never found.' But, of course, they'd crumbled away, you see they do that when they're burned."

Black pearls are so rare that many legends and perhaps some wishful thinking has surrounded stories about them.

Bill Abernethy:
"Mary, Queen of Scots, had several necklaces and brooches in Scotch pearls and I think it was Lord Darnley that stole her jewellery and sold it. But she also had a necklace of black pearls which is very rare, black pearls are very few and far between you know. But you do get black pearls and at that time, as you know, the rivers were full of pearls here and it wasn't any great difficulty to get a few necklaces together but to get a black necklace was a different story. The black ones had probably been saved up for Mary, Queen of Scots, and it was made into a necklace. When she was taken to England and her jewellery was either stolen or confiscated and whether it was broken up and sold or not. . . . But the story goes that the black necklace of pearls was bought in a junk shop in Aberdeen away back at the beginning of this century for two shillings and sixpence. That was the story that went about. The boy that bought them for two shillings and sixpence knew the value, he was a pearl fisher from Stirling, that's all I can tell you about it. Where they went to after that, I don't know but that's the story, whether it's true or no, you've just got to take it at its face value."

ISHBEL MACLEAN

DAVID COLVILLE & SONS LTD
(GLENGARNOCK WORKS)
Nº 2 Blast Furnace
27-1-21

Glengarnock Steel

On 21st December 1978, steel was made in Glengarnock, north Ayrshire, for the last time: its owners, the British Steel Corporation, had deemed the open hearth furnaces there to be obsolescent, a decision ratified by the Government.

On that day, just prior to the final charging of the last furnace in operation — the 'H' — four of its team scrawled their names alongside one of its five doors. Time has already partially erased their signatures but the informed onlooker, stopping to ponder over the reasoning behind such an action, does not take long to come to a conclusion: these men wanted it to be known that they had witnessed the demise of the open hearth process in Britain. They were the last link in what had become, over the past eighty-six years at Glengarnock, a traditional industry. But before steel had been produced in Glengarnock there had been iron. The laying of the Glasgow/Ayr railway in 1840 dispelled any doubts that local industrialists James Merry, Alexander Allison and Alexander Cunninghame may have had as to the viability of an ironworks on the shores of Kilbirnie Loch. If supplies of coal, iron and limestone in the area were to run out then these raw materials could thereafter be easily imported. More importantly, the pig iron produced could be quickly dispatched.

Thus by 1843 eight blast furnaces were producing iron which found its way to Europe and America. As these markets began to make their own iron and the supply of local ironstone became exhausted, the company, now owned by John Charles Cunninghame, son of the original founder, and his cousin John Cunninghame, decided that the time had come to make steel. Four eight-ton Bessemer converters were installed (1885-1920) and seven years later, in 1892, the first of the open hearth furnaces was built followed closely by a rolling mill and a structural department.

Over the years a variety of products were to be dispatched from the works: pig iron, shells (during the First World War), rails, sleepers, fish plates, joists, angles, tees, channels, bars, blooms, slabs and flats.

The establishment of an iron and, eventually, steel works at Glengarnock attracted men from far and near. For not only was there the chance of male employment: the thread and net works and woollen mills of the neighbouring town of Kilbirnie and Dalry

Blast furnace workers–date unknown (probably late 1920s).

Above: Furnace workers, c. 1921. Opposite: Lithuanian women and children in Glengarnock.

proffered work for their womenfolk. Not surprisingly, families from Ireland, England, Spain (from where much of the ore for Glengarnock's iron furnaces was eventually imported), Italy, Poland and Lithuania were attracted to this industrial pocket of essentially rural Ayrshire.

Robert Whitelaw:

"Mother came from Workington—a sort of steel working community, too. I presume the works was slack there and they came up here when the steelwork was being enlarged and more people came into it. They came from Workington in the 1890s—her mother and five of the family came up here for the work."

Joe McAuley (second generation Lithuanian):

"When they came to a certain age they had to go into the Russian Army. And father had a brother in the army; and when he was home he says, 'Brother, if there's anything you can do to avoid the army, do anything at all. Because really, the conditions is really not too pleasant.' So the result wis father made up his mind: he came over here to Scotland.

"Well, it was just farming [in Lithuania]. Ah'll tell ye the way they lived then: they had a small holding an' whitever grun they cultivated there it was for their own use, for the winter. And then if they had a pig, a sheep and a horse—if they had a surplus— they ta'en it tae the market. And they worked sorta on a barter system: they exchanged jist for something that they really required.

"There was no schooling there. None o' them got

any schooling. Mother—if she was takin' note o' anything—used to sit and draw strokes tae she came tae ten. And then she put a top on ten and she went along until she had another ten."

Laura Buchanan:

"I can remember them [Lithuanians, known locally as 'Poles'] coming off the train because it was a local man in the steelwork who met them aw—he was a foreman there or a manager. They couldn't say a word of English that I remember. And they all had tickets on their backs [saying Glengarnock, Ayrshire] when they came off the train. They seemed all to come just in one batch. The men came first. Ah don't remember when their wives came. But they did come. And they had big families after they came here, quite a lot o' them."

Many Ayrshire men, too, sought a start in the steel works, regarding it as an attractive alternative to life down the local pits.

John Ramsay:

"Instead of going to the pit that first morning, ah went to the steelwork; and sat and waited till the manager passed me. Ah chased up the manager and asked him for a job. He took me tae a foreman that already said he didn't require anybody, told him to start me. After Ah'd worked a short time, till about nine o'clock, the foreman came to me and says, 'You didn't tell me that you worked in the pit.' Ah says, 'It's quite obvious if you look at me.' Ah never worked any place else—at that time still

having on my yorks or knee strings. 'So why did you leave the pit and come here?' So ah says, 'Wait.' And ah pulled up ma shirt at the back. He says, 'You're supposed to go back to the pit, ah'll have tae send you back.' But when he looked at ma back he says, 'You're going back to no pit.'

"Ah was skinned from the hips up to the back of the neck. The company that owned the pits also owned the steelwork and they were very economic with their rails down the pit. And time and again the hutch would jump the road and you had to lift these hutches on. And the only method of doing it was turning your back on the hutch, putting in a spragg to hold it in position. Then you put your back against it and heaved it on to the road. Your back got skinned from the neck right down to the buttocks. Ah never saw a drawer with anything else but a skinned back. And, well, that's the reason that the engineer foreman decided ah wasn't going back to the pits."

With such an influx of people (in 1841 Kilbirnie's population totalled 2,631, in 1851 it was 5,484 and by 1901 it was 7,207) the hamlet of Glengarnock which hitherto contained very little more than an inn and Kilbirnie's station, mushroomed. Families settled not only along its Main Street but within the steelworks site itself in rows upon rows of single-storey houses, serviced by the company store and its celebrated liquor annexe, the 'Billy Ruffin' (the local interpretation of 'Bellorophone', after the famous British warship that took Napoleon to exile in St. Helena).

Although working conditions regarding safety improved with time, older hands still referred to the works as the 'Slaughterhouse'. The following account concerns the Bessemer plant where air was blown through holes in the bottom of the cupolas into molten iron, initially causing slag and molten metal to be thrown out rather violently.

Joe Smith:

"Ma faither wis brought home. He was burnt—claes were burnt aff him. See, when you're drawing in these bogeys from the vessel—ken, a cupola—slag keeps bubbling and this yin must have been right full up. Ken, the wye it bubbles oot and it caught alight and they took him hame. Ah think they took him hame in a cab, a horse-drawn cab, aye. An' he come in—oh, he wis an awfae state. And would you believe the treatment he got efter that—ah remember—leeches pit on his back—leeches! And whenever they were full they were pit intae salt so they would vomit up their thingmae so they'd be used again and then pit intae a jar. This wis a doctor's idea. Aye, they did that wi' leeches, ken—burns—bad burns. Ah seen it—ah seen as much as three leeches on his back— his bare back. He was quite a bit aff before he was right again fur workin'. But he wouldnae need tae be right better. It was as quick as he could get out tae work because there were nae money. Ah don't know whether we wur gettin' any compensation.

Blast furnaces and pig beds (taken from a supplement to 'The Metal Industry', 3rd June 1927).

Ah think aw he got was a lift fae the workmates—ken, subscribin'."

The attitude of the private owners of Glengarnock Steelworks as to sanitary conditions was not portrayed in an enthusiastic manner by their former employees. Until the erection of amenity blocks at the Mill and Melting Shops in the 'fifties and 'sixties respectively, washing-up facilities were very basic and the men had to take their meal breaks alongside their work.

John Williamson:
"They had wee cabins built in the Melting Shop and that's where everybody had to eat. And to make tea, you had to put a steel plate in the furnace, heat it, and boil your can. That's how you made your tea. And you just sat beside your job and ate. And if there was a lot of dust, well, you just absorbed the dust along wi' your meal. It helped to fill a hole. . . . The modern worker would lay an egg if he saw the way we worked in these days. You got a two-and-a-half gallon zinc-coated pail and you filled that with water and that hung on a hook outside the cabin, open to the atmosphere and open to all the coke and alloy dust that fell around it. And that was the water that you drank—that was the water you made your tea with."

Andrew Dick:
"Well, ye got bits o' scrap—flat—ones that ye could lift. Ye'd tae throw them intae the door o' the furnace—into the bay, an' pull them out when they wis hot and put them up on a couple of bricks and used that. Ye toasted in below that. And ye'd get your [tea] drum, an old syrup tin, an' boiled it that way."

George Barclay:
"As far as washing-up when yir day was finished as many as possible got around about the one washhand basin, an old sink and a cold tap goin' intae it.
"There were no hot water facilities. If you got hot water, you were fortunate. Because it meant you were working outside the shop someplace. You were at the Mill and you got a bloom end and ye got an ordinary bucket and you put it on the top o' it till the water was warm. And that was you—you had warm water tae wash your hands at the end o' yir shift."

James Vann:
"The sanitaries were open, were dry closets. That's what they were, aye. Like a lot of canaries in a tin box, aye!"

The tremendous heat and heavy nature of the work required special clothes.

George Blair:
"Well, they [melters at the open hearth furnaces] wore the blue flannel pants and shirts—that was to take the sweat, and the wee cap. Fireman's caps, they called them—they were just a thin black material. Well, you'd mibbae jist go in wi' a new one an' go in some place where there was heat and—pssssst—it was burnt!
"Ah used tae go down tae the store and get the hand leathers. They were good. They must've been about six inches b'eight: they jist cut a nice slit and jist slipped their hand through. So that was protection [for the palm of the hand].
"The melters wore a white scarf—that was a sweat rag. You had always that tae wipe—you know, you wis gettin' blinded whiles wi' sweat. Because if you wis working, it was running off your broo.
"We wore a canvas apron: you had it down below yir knees an' it protected against any burns or splashes."

William Dubordieu (second man at one of Glengarnock's iron blast furnaces):
"You'd tae take two shirts wi' ye when you were workin'. When you were bye wi' the one, you ta'en it off and pit oan a dry one, blue flannel shirts, they ate up the sweat, y'see. Then we had a thing we pulled over wur boots to save wur boots tae gettin' burnt, we were in hot sand [pig beds were moulded in sand]. They were jist made of the beltin' offa the different machinery and wooden soles and you nailed it roon aboot; and then you laced it roon your boot. And that done tae ye wur bye wi' the cast. But you werenae long in takin' them oaf after you were bye wi' them. You couldnae walk aboot wi' them, you know—you could have tripped."

Wanda Mackaveetch (daughter of a pig lifter at the blast furnaces):
"They had t'get moleskin trousers. They were thick, thick, thick. . . . They needed something to keep the heat out of their legs. Because when they went to their work they wore long johns—drawers we called them. They never wore socks, they got white linen, usually, and they rolled it round their feet and all round their legs and they pulled their drawers down to there [ankle]. That's the way they went to their work—no socks, wi' the moleskin trousers.
"They were expensive then, too. You coulda got an ordinary pair of trousers cheaper, but the men had t' get those."

Work, however, was not always available in the area: the slumps and booms of heavy industry were felt keenly in Glengarnock, a village that lived by and for steel. When jobs were scarce, families would move on to hopefully more secure climes.

Matt Yuill:
"At the end of the nineteenth century, many families, when work was slack, went off to the

U.S.A. to work in the pits there. If trade got better in Scotland, many returned. My mother recalled—as a little girl sailing back to Scotland up the Clyde—the families sat in the hatches, tidying up before they reached the tail of the bank. I last saw my Grandma going off to America—her seventh crossing of the 'Herring Pond', the Atlantic Ocean. This seems to convey to me the idea that, ach, it wasn't very big: it was just a pond. You know, you just went across."

John Ramsay:

"Dalry men were generally known as Chinks. That's supposed to have originated from somebody that had emigrated to Waterbury, a favourite place for Dalry people before the development o' the motor industry in America. And there'd been a queue at this employment gate in Waterbury where they made watches and there was a Chinaman in it, also a Dalry man. When they got up to the employment office—there had been quite a few refusals—the official asked this man, 'Where do you come from?' 'Ah come from Dalry.' 'Oh, come in.' Started right away. So they asked the Chinaman next. He says, 'Me Dalry man, too!' So he got started as well! And that's how Dalry men are supposed to have got the nickname, Chinamen."

Ironically, it was war—the Great War—that was to bring expansion and prosperity to Glengarnock Works. David Colville and Sons of Motherwell, backed by Ministry of Munitions money, refurbished the ailing furnaces and built a new open hearth melting shop and a rolling mill. By 1919, 3,000 were employed, the highest labour force ever recorded.

The village of Glengarnock grew in confidence during such a thriving time: the friendly rivalry that always existed between its inhabitants and those of Kilbirnie, on the other side of the Garnock River, became more evident.

Ellen McConachie and Helen Kennedy:

"Ye put the links [chain by which a pot, etc. hangs over a fire from the 'crook' or iron hook] on as you needed: drew them forrit as you needed—an' whatever size you needed.

"They used tae say that wis why the kettle never biled in Kilbirnie. For they had it on the top link!"

While Glengarnock was dominated by steel, its inhabitants were, in the main, only first generation industrial workers: most still had an affinity for the country and rural skills could be relied upon when money was scarce.

John Ramsay:

"Ma father was what was known as a good pot filler. He could turn his hand to get a rabbit or wild duck or 'cushies' or wood pigeons, they're better known as. One night he said to me, 'Come on, Ah know where there's a hare feedin'.' And he

Jock Ramsay outside his home in Kilbirnie.

lifted a net, and we went away up this road to a gate. He put the net on a gate and he says to me, 'Now, when the hare comes into that net, get it, break its neck.' Well, Ah looked at him. Ah says, 'Listen, don't tell me that a hare's gonnae run intae a net on a gate when there's only an occasional bush round that field along wi' a wire fence.' He says to me, 'Just you lie there and when it comes in the net, get it, ah'm telling ye.'

"And away he went down to the bottom of the field and ah could hear him rattling two stones together he'd picked up. Sure as he said it the hare come running up and stopped aboot ten or fifteen yards from the gate, looked round, then it dived through the bars of the gate into the net and it let out a squeal. Well, ah was a bit soft-hearted and ah put ma hand in and got the hare b' the ears and threw it out behind me and away it went quite happy, ah suppose.

"And he came up. 'Where is it?' he says.

"Ah says, 'Where's whit?'

" 'Where's the hare?'

" 'Ah never seen any hare.'

" 'You're a damned liar,' he says, 'the hare went intae that net.'

"Ah says, 'Naw it didnae. Ah never seen any hare.'

" 'Listen,' he says, 'this is your education: when a hare gets disturbed in a field where it's feeding at night, it'll go through nothing else but a place where there's a gate. And that hare went intae that net, ah don't care whit ye say.'

"Well, he was right!

"Another time, ah saw him sitting stringing horse hair through ears of corn. Ah never asked him any questions, ah just watched him. And when he had quite a bundle o' these horse hairs strung corn, he says, 'Come on.' And he took me up tae this field where there was cushies feedin'. There was a plantin' run alongside it. Well, naturally, the cushies got up when we went up and we went along the edge o' this plantin' and scattered this corn and then hid. Well, in a short time the cushies went back down to feed and ah saw a few of them begin tae flutter their wings and give a jump and when there was half a dozen like this, he says, 'That'll do.'

"And we went along and picked up the cushies. They couldn't fly because the horse hair had entangled their wings—the corn was over their gullet but there wur plenty of horse hair trailing behind tae entangle their wings and they couldn't fly. That was another way of getting cushies!"

Such escapades must have provided welcome relief—as well as welcome food during hard times—for those forced to live literally on the job. The Long Row, the Front Row, the Square, the Pond Row (next to the reservoirs containing water for the works' steam engines), the Coal Lye, the Store Row and the Railway Cottages were sandwiched between furnaces, slag heaps and railway lines.

Sanitary arrangements within the 'Raws' (Rows) were primitive: drinking water was got from pillar wells, outside toilets were shared one per three households and, unlike the later works' houses—the 'Hill' and the inaptly named Cornpark—there were no wash houses. Slop water was thrown into sheughs, open channels which ran alongside the houses' front doors to a common sewer; and household rubbish was deposited in 'mickeys', or ashpits, nearby.

Joe McAuley:
"Well, when we wis goin' to bed, if wur feet wis dirty and that, we sat on this sheugh and washed wur feet and got prepared there for bed."

Helen Kennedy:
"In yir entry wis where ye kept yer pail o' clean water and yer basin to wash in. There was a lovely, big barrel on a stand outside. And we collected the rain water in it: and you washed your face wi' the rain water. In winter there were ice floatin' roon aboot an' it hit the side o' yir basin an' tinkled all roon aboot." [shivers]

Large families crowded into rooms and kitchens in the labyrinth of homes situated within the works or in the village of Glengarnock itself where conditions were only marginally better. Thus there was room for only the bare essentials of furniture: belongings, as well as coal, had to be stored under set-in beds in many cases.

Joe Smith:
"We had three in-set beds. Ma father and mother slept in the kitchen—the big wan in the kitchen—and we slept whit they cawed the 'jail'! Part a it would be shown tae the kitchen, like, and the rest

o' it would be in between the room and the kitchen. The other bed was jist the full length, ken; it was curtained tae.

"Aw, ye had tae have curtains. There was nae privacy, ye had tae have yur claes on a chair near the bed. . . .

"You used to have neighbours in. Sometimes you couldnae come oot a bed till they went away! Ken, they wid blether away there! But if you were in the room it was a different thing. Well, the girls were in the room—three girls were in the room."

Joe McAuley:
"There was no mattresses in thae days. They made a big, big tick; and we went over to the farm and we got straw and they filled this tick wi' straw and they put it on the bed. And that's what you lay on. That was ma mattress. But the cushions was good aw the same because they was always feathers. Mother, every Christmas, she would buy either a goose or a duck or a drake or something like that and she would pook the feathers off it and she would save these feathers and then put them intae cushions. But wur covering was good. It was a big tick and it was filled wi' feathers—just like a continental quilt. Well, this is what we covered wurselves wi'. And it was warm."

Helen Kennedy:
"We hud a meal and a flooer [flour] girnal [meal chest]. Ma mother goat it as a weddin' present: she worked as a farm servant at a farm at the Longbar [next to the steelworks, now a housing estate]—that's a long time ago. And the one side held a bag o' meal and the other a bag o' flour. And in below held things for bakin'."

But there was no doubt at all that in such cramped surroundings a housewife's pride and joy was her dresser.

Ellen McConachie:
"Like a sideboard, but it had two doors. And then abin that were wir three drawers wi' glass handles on them. And then there wir a big rack and this rack hid like wee shelves wi' bars across an' we hud plates in it: a big plate and two wee'er yins like would haud a turkey nooadays—kinna Willow pattern. An then at this place where the wee drawers were there wir mibbae two or three ither plates—if ye wir lucky enough t' hiv what matched. And if they didnae match, well, that was alright—you made them fancy!

"And we hud mibbae a hauf a set o' cheeny: an' if ye wur lucky enough ye hud twa hauf sets. And sittin' on the flat bit, we hud a pair o' wally dugs an' whit they would cry noo a fruit thing. It wis kinna crystally—cut gless, likely it would be. An' a photae o' yur lawd or yir swank!

"Ye've seen a jug and ewer? Well, we hud two o' that—jist sittin' up beside this gless thing; and sittin' beside that wis the two wally dugs."

Glengarnock's good fortune after the 1914-18 war was to be short lived. The miners' strikes of the 'twenties and the emerging worldwide economic recession spelled hardship for its steelwork families. The works' owners had to introduce a programme of rationalisation: in 1930 the emerging company of Colvilles Ltd., under the direction of Sir John Craig, designated Glengarnock as a producer of structural steel. The works' structural department, producing in the main girders (hence the local name still used, the 'Girder Shop') took on a more sophisticated image: five years later it pioneered electric arc welding. Such a development was introduced, however, at the cost of Glengarnock's blast iron furnaces: these were closed down in 1930 as iron production was now to be concentrated within Clyde Iron Works. As a result, families began to move away from the area in the vain hope that work could be had elsewhere for by now Britain was in the grip of the Depression. In 1933 only one furnace was in operation in Glengarnock and some families lived on 'broo money' for nigh on five years (1930-35).

The food a family eats is a good indication of the financial circumstances it is experiencing. In Glengarnock, like everywhere else, good fare was enjoyed when business was booming—a pig lifter would enjoy a breakfast of half a pound of bacon and half a dozen eggs or eat two pounds of steak in one sitting. But the lasting memories of food, like those that follow, are held by people who know what it is like to go wanting.

James Jennings:
"It used to be an occasion when all the men in the area would walk over the Fairlie Moor from Dalry. Ye knew when they came back, that you were gonnae get fish for your dinner because this was them goin' over to Fairlie, to the boats, to try and scrounge some fish fae the fishermen who were comin' in. We used to say, 'That's ma Daddy away to Fairlie. We'll get fish. . . .'

"And you could rest assured, on the way back, they'd be into a potato field or a turnip field. And this was how they lived. They would go out in the middle of the night and scrounge things. Those days made, no' necessarily criminals, but offenders, out of people who otherwise wouldn't have resorted to that type of thing. Because they had families to feed. . . ."

Ellen McConachie:
"Tatties and dab at the still [stool]. . . . Well, on a winter night or a winter day yer mother had a big poat o' tatties bilin' ready, sittin' up oan the hob. Aye, it was a big stane poat—no' enamel, ken—it wis too cauld.

"So oot come the stool—nae cover [tablecloth] on it—jist oot come the stool an' a saucer o' salt. An' ye got yer potato—lifted a potato and peeled the skin oaf it and ye dabbed it in the salt an' ye ate it. If ye liked, ye cud get a wee bit butter tae it.

Opposite: Railway cottages on site at Glengarnock works.

"Mibbae it wis yer tea, mibbae it wis yer dinner—jist as it suited."

The harsh dictates of the Means Test caused many people to perjure themselves in order to get a reasonable income for their families:

John Dempsey:
"Well, we come onto the Means Test and this is where ma father and ma mother got the hard en' o' it. Because whenever we got a job in the Guide Mill, ma father didn't get anything. He was unemployed and we were supposed t' keep ma father. If ah worked for three month, then he got nothing—which forced us t' say, 'We've left the house.' Ma eldest brother was married so we'd all say, 'We're living with ma brother.' That was to get something from the Labour Exchange when we weren't working; and something for ma father to get because he couldn't say that we were in the house keepin' him."

The ramifications of the Means Test were to have violent repercussions in Kilbirnie: on a February night in 1931, the Riot Act was read. Local Communist leaders, backed by Glasgow members of the National Unemployed Workers' Movement and contingents of supporters from nearby Beith and Dalry, as well as Glengarnock, had marched to the town's Walker Hall where local councillors were holding a meeting.

Dick Sneddon:
"Well, the street was black from the Masonic Hall to the Walker Hall; and black on the ither side, right to the bridge. Oh, the crowd in front o' the Walker Hall was massive. . . . It was night, ah would say aroon aboot half-past seven we'd actually land there. Now the demonstration, ah suppose, would be advertised aforehand. Well, the councillors must have asked the policemen t' be there that night. There must've been oh, hundreds o' policemen between the Commercial Hotel and the Walker Hall—*in* the building.

"The deputation came out and said that the answer wisnae satisfactory. . . . Now the Riot Act, it seems, wis read inside the building. It seems that someb'dy hud come out—the policeman concerned—and the Riot Act was then read. . . . But ah've always mind o' the strap [of helmet] comin' down—the inspector—and that must've been the sign for them tae draw their batons. . . . Well, ah don't know whit made me bury ma head in among the crowd—you know the way it all broke up—but ah've always mind o' gettin' this blow on the shoulder and then taps. . . . Ah wus frightened, aye, very frightened! Ah think everybody wis frightened. Ah mean, the people o' Kilbirnie had never seen anythin' like that in their life before! There wurnae one person armed in that demonstration because there were wimmen in it—an' children—wi' wee prams."

Main Street, Glengarnock–looking eastwards towards Glengarnock Railway Station.

George Henderson:

"Communists are not born: they're bred. And to this day in Kilbirnie you have Communists who were converted at that time."

It was to take another World War—the 1939-45—to remedy the situation: steel is a crucial commodity during such a time and Glengarnock steel was to be used in shipbuilding. The men began to go back to work. . . .

Helen Kennedy:

"Ma husband was goin' oot t' his work this Thursday night—two tae ten—he hid goat three shifts—goat three days broo an' three shifts an' this wis marvellous. Well, when you goat the three shifts, the week before that you only goat three days broo which was twelve and six. Well, that had t' do ye t' the next again Friday. 'Ah've fill't a [football] coupon in the paper,' he says. 'It'll only cost fourpence haepenny t' send it away. Will ye post it fur me?' Ah sayed, 'Oh, alright, ah'll see.'

"So away he went tae his work an' ah says, 'Oh, my, that coupon t' post. Ah've fourpence haepenny. Fourpence haepenny would get me three eggs in the mornin'. Ah don't know whit t' dae!' An' ah didnae know whit tae dae. An' ah waited an' ah waited an' wunnert what ah wid dae. Ah says, 'Och, him an' his coupons. Ah'll jist buy three eggs!'

"So on the Saturday he wis checkin' his coupon. His coupon come up. It wis mibbae a hundred and forty [pounds], ah cunnae hae mind. Bit it wis quite a loat a money. Oh, me! He nivir spoke t' me for three weeks efter it. Oh, ah wis cut, ah wis upset!

An' he says, 'Ah asked ye t' post that coupon!' Ah says, 'Ah know you asked me t' post the coupon but you'd a hud no breakfast nor neither wid the weans hiv had a breakfast if ah hud posted that coupon.' Well, he come roon an' he says, 'Oh, right enough, it mibbae wid a went doon'."

After 1945, hand-to-mouth existence was no longer paramount and the steelwork families began to find more time for leisure. More money meant more sophisticated activities were enjoyed but some, like the two that follow, gained momentum and still survive today.

Anna Williamson:

"I can remember it was an all-night sitting before the [Kilbirnie] Flower Show. And my cousin and I used to get the Friday afternoon off school to go and gather rushes. We would gather armfuls of rushes and they were all put into these vases and whipped off! The rushes were used for floral art, as you might say—to hold the flowers in position. But in the morning, when everything was ready, they had the Co-op coal cart—horse and cart—and it was the joy of our life if we were the one that was picked to sit and hold something steady on the cart. But more often I seemed to be the one that had to walk up carrying something—which wasn't quite so nice, you know. My father tried all sorts of gadgets. His whole life was flowers. But the garden wasn't a thing of beauty. The garden was full of wee boxes covering the flowers to keep them clean! If we got an east wind from the steelwork—sometimes at the weekend—I don't know what they did but there was a great deal of pollution came. And I've seen him heartbroken if he had something not covered and it got dirty."

Joe Smith:

"We were wans fur fitba—day and night. Ah've seen us goan' fur wur tea and comin' back. . . . The gemm was on. You just got in a gemm. You hud tae get a partner fur the opposite side. It would start wi' abit mibbae, say five or six at the start on each side and then b' the end a it they'd be very near twenty-two on each side! But they had always tae get another wan tae go on the opposite side: and the gemm would go on tae night and we were wans fur bed."

By the 'fifties, however, two major local authority housing estates were built in Kilbirnie and the drift of Glengarnock families to more modern homes outside the village began. Their going spelled the beginning of the end for the community. Of the five Co-op departments, three public houses, eleven shops, a licensed grocer and two banks, only a hairdresser, the licensed grocer, a sub-post office/newsagent, a public house and a social club remain today. Not that the loyalty of some of Glengarnock's inhabitants was easily dissuaded.

Jackie Clark:

"Ah still think that this village of Glengarnock is due a better destiny than what it's getting. There's nothing to me to beat a village life and some people come into ma shop that I haven't seen for a long, long and weary and the first thing they say, 'Well, poor Glengarnock! But if there was a house built in Glengarnock, ah would come back to it tomorrow.'

"Let us restore places where we used to be and fill the gap sites. Ah organised a petition and a thousand signed to try and do something about the village of Glengarnock. And the authorities stated that the people who signed this didn't belong to Glengarnock. The petition was left to people who came into my shop and, after all, it's only a wee village shop. Ah had people who came from all over, visiting the steelworks, travellers, people who belong to Glengarnock, people who had emigrated abroad who'd come back to Glengarnock who said,

'In the name of heavens, what's happened to this place?'

"We've had to look at dilapidation for so many years that we really had to do something. I erected a cross—a ten-foot cross—and on that cross was, 'GLENGARNOCK, DIED OF NEGLECT'."

Although the village of Glengarnock had begun to run down, the works continued to be the major employer in the Garnock Valley (Glengarnock, Kilbirnie, Dalry, Beith and Lochwinnoch). In 1968, following extensive alterations to its rolling mill, it was taken over by the British Steel Corporation. But, basically, the open hearth furnaces remained as they had been after the First World War. Newer, quicker, more efficient processes, coupled with marked foreign competition and a fall in the demand for steel, contributed to the demise of the Glengarnock Melting Shop in 1978. A reduced rolling mill operation, employing just over 200 people, has continued, its survival due to the establishment of the 'Glengarnock Agreement' which promotes job flexibility—something which would never have been tolerated a few years before.

However, recent figures show increased productivity there and hopes are high that more hands may be taken on in 1982. This cannot be soon enough for the 31 per cent at present unemployed in the Valley.

Government authorities are valiantly trying to introduce new industries to the area but those firms which have been attracted by specially built premises and financial incentives are still in embryo, employing relatively few local people. The future is bleak.

Helen Kennedy:

"It's jist history repeatin' itself. It is. Because wir lifeblood was the steelwork an' the [iron] furnaces. An' when the furnaces closed down, there was a loat went away. And there the steelworks is the same an' they're goin' away because the steelworks is closed doon. It's jist a tragedy. An' an older body, seein' it happenin', it's jist heartbreakin'. Because you were intendin' t' bring up yer grandchildren in the area. They'll need to go away fae here t' look for work—if they can get it ither places. Where in Scotland are they goin' t' get it?"

LORNA LEWIS

Derelict melting shop in winter 1979/80.

Clan Neil of Barra

"The McNeills originally came from Ireland and they used to say in Gaelic 'Clann Neill nam piob's nam breacan sibh a thug a chreach a Eirinn'—Clan Neil of the pipes and tartan that came from Ireland to raid and stayed."
—Nan McKinnon

Lying as it does at the southernmost end of the Outer Hebrides, Barra has never been the most easily accessible of islands. The advent of air travel has helped to alter this, but for most, the journey from Oban to Castlebay by sea, is still one of some five hours—when a direct route is taken by MacBraynes ferries and when the weather is favourable. The island of Barra and its adjacent islands of Vatersay and Mingulay have successfully retained Gaelic culture and identity where other islands have been swamped by the tide of outside influences. This is probably due to a number of factors. Firstly, the island's relative isolation in geographical terms. Secondly, and related to this, the close-knit nature of the community. Thirdly, Barra's adherence to the Catholic faith, which, along with the islands of South Uist and Eriskay, gave it a sense of separate identity from the other islands of the Hebrides. It also spared the island the cultural ravages of over-zealous Presbyterianism which destroyed Gaelic oral and musical tradition in other areas of Scotland. Therefore, while the historical experience of Barra, and the history of Clan Neil, shares much in common with that of other Highland areas and clans, the survival of a lively, comparatively unbroken oral tradition has given the island something of a closer affinity with the past. Through this we are fortunate in being able to glean some idea of the clan days, not from the history book, but from the passing of oral tradition from generation to generation through the centuries.

The McNeills of Barra are undoubtedly of very ancient lineage. Martin Martin writing in 1695 tells us that according to the genealogists of his day, the chief of the McNeills was the thirty-fourth of his name who had possessed Barra in unbroken descent. The Old Statistical Account states that the McNeills originally came from Ireland, related to the O'Neills of Ulster, and that they were in possession of Barra before the 'Danes'. It is at least certain that they were there during the Norse occupation of the Hebrides. Niall of the Nine Hostages who ruled at Tara in Ireland from 308 to 405 is commonly regarded as the progenitor of the clan. It is believed that his ancestor 'Niall of the Castle' came to Barra around 1030 as vassal to the King of Norway and married one of his daughters, his progeny remaining in feudal homage to the Norwegian Crown until 1266.

Other Clan historians, however, have held that the progenitor was a norseman named 'Njal'—McNeill being the same as Nilsson—perhaps Njal of the race of Ketil Flatneb who ruled the Hebrides during the tenth century. What is important, however, is that they held identity from a common progenitor and that as an established clan in Scotland we can go back no further than the eleventh century. The construction of the original Keep of Castle Kisimul probably began around the same period. In Scotland the McNeills of Barra have always been regarded as chiefs of the clan, above the cadet branches found in Gigha and Knapdale. The traditional clan lands were the islands of Barra, Vatersay, Mingulay and all the islands south to Barra Head, but as late as the seventeenth century the McNeills were in possession of part of South Uist, before being driven out by the McDonalds of Clanranald at the battle of North Boisdale in 1601. During the clan period they feature as allies of the McLeans of Duart and links between the clans were close.

Under the clan system the relationship between the chief and his clan, in Barra as elsewhere, was a well-defined one, what has been described as a 'mixture of autocracy and communism'.

Roderick McNeill:
"They were like one family. The chief had to

Above: Kisimul Castle. Opposite: Barra from Vatersay.

allocate the land and the fishing banks as well. He also had to arrange marriages and generally to order the lives of all his people. Where one of his men was in rather dire straits, for example if twins were born in a family, one of the pair was taken into the castle and brought up there as one of McNeill's own family."

McNeill's responsibilities also extended to replacement of cattle lost by tenants and admission to the castle of those with no family who had grown too old to look after themselves. The arranging of marriages was an important duty of the chief as Martin Martin discovered in Barra in 1695:

"When a tenant's wife in this or adjacent islands dies, he then addresses himself to McNeill of Barra representing his loss and at the same time desires

Sixteenth-century graveslab showing Hebridean birlinn.

that he would be pleased to recommend a wife to him. Upon this representation McNeill finds out a suitable match for him and the woman's name being told him immediately he goes to her carrying with him a bottle of strong waters for their entertainment at marriage, which is then consummated."

The paternalism of the chiefs extended to a responsibility for discipline.

Archie McDonald:
"The McNeill had a day every year for judging what happened through the whole year. If there was any crime of any description they [the clanspeople] would have to come forward and he was giving judgement—what would be if there was any punishment or anything like that, and it was always on horseback. He was always sitting in his saddle over at a place on the west side of Barra called 'Judgement Seat'. The site is still there. If there was anything wrong it was always put straight, on a straight tack and the rules were laid down to them."

Rent to the McNeills was paid in kind, in military service and in produce such as corn or livestock.

Roderick McNeill:
"The islands to the south of Vatersay—they were all inhabited at that time, paid their rent in kind—wool and birds' feathers and no doubt oil and the actual flesh of the birds. There was one bird that was regarded as a particular delicacy, the *fachaich*. The *fachaich* is the young of the puffin. They were paid as part of the rent. Now the place where this rent was delivered called Port an taigh mhal can still be seen at a place called Nask."

The people of Mingulay and the other islands where the fachaich was harvested do not seem to have used ropes as they did on St Kilda, but clambered among the rocks like goats.

The esteem with which the McNeill was held, in Barra at least, was humorously referred to by James Wilson in his *Voyage Round the Coasts of Scotland*, published in 1842. There Wilson relates that in ancient times the custom was for the herald to sound a horn from the battlements of Castle Kisimul and proclaim 'Hear ye people and nations listen, the great McNeill of Barra having finished his meal, the princes and kings of the earth may dine'—a good story which the historical sceptic should not judge too harshly.

Tales of the clan days are told by the older people on the island with familiarity, as if a centuries-old event had occurred but a few years previously. Not surprisingly, the Barra men have been noted for their seamanship from earliest times, and the fortunes of the Barra people have always been inextricably bound up with the sea. The sight of McNeill's Galleys or 'Birlinns' as they were called, setting off on a raid, was a familiar one in the olden days.

Cattle on the beach at Vatersay.

Archie McDonald:

"Oh, they were great pirates, they could manage that. There were no use of them trying to get a hold of them on the high seas."

Ruaraidh the Tartar, chief of the McNeills from 1598 to 1622, seems to have been particularly notorious in this respect, and was none too scrupulous in means of adding to his revenue. He was comparatively safe as long as he confined his attentions to French or Dutch vessels but he extended his piracy to the coasts of Ireland where he looted an English vessel and spread such terror that his exploits came to the attention of Queen Elizabeth who complained strongly to King James VI of Scots.

Roderick McNeill:

"King James summoned Ruaraidh but he did not obey. He was kidnapped by McKenzie of Kintail who brought him to Edinburgh. His defence to the King for his action then, was that he was merely avenging the King's own mother who had been beheaded at the orders of Queen Elizabeth. James thought it politic to let him go!"

Raids by the Hebrideans on Shetland, and Orkney in particular, were frequent, the largest invasion of Orkney taking place in 1460. It is told in contemporary accounts how the Hebrideans burned, plundered and ravaged the country, massacred the inhabitants without regard to sex or age, and carried off whatever cattle or other property they could lay their hands on.

Nan McKinnon tells of one raid by the Barra men on Shetland and of 'Gille Dubh Thangasdail'.

Nan McKinnon:

"McNeill wanted to go to Shetland for a raid—they used to raid one another and take all the cattle and sheep and everything. Anyway, McNeill took Gille Dubh Thangasdail with him. Gille Dubh was a strong young man, the only son of a widow that lived down at Tangasdail. He was the strongest man in Barra and McNeill was afraid of Gille Dubh. The chief of the Shetlanders at that time was a man named the 'Bauch Sealltainneach'. He was called the 'Bauch' because of the style of his whiskers—the bauch is the male goat. 'Now,' says McNeill, 'if the Bauch Sealltainneach is getting the better of me, you take my side, but if I'm getting

Fliuch An Oidhche

Steadily

Chuala mi'n de, hu il o — ro Sgeul nach b'ait leam, o hi i ibh o

Gun tug Clann Neill, hu il o — ro Dru-im a' chu-ain orr', boch oi — rinn o.

Gun tug Clann Neill, hu il oro
Druim a' chuain orr', o hi i ibh o
Luchd nan seol ard, hu hil oro
'S na long luatha, boch oirinn o.

Luchd nan seol ard, hu il oro,
'S na long luatha, o hi i ibh o
Nam brataichean, hu il oro
Dearg is uaine, boch oirinn o.

'S nam brataichean, hu il oro
Dearg is uaine, o hi i ibh o
'S iomadh bairneach, hu il oro
Glas a ghluais iad, boch oirinn o.

'S iomadh bairneach, hu il oro
Glas a ghluais iad, o hi i ibh o
Agus duileasg, hu il oro
Donn a bhuain iad, boch oirinn o

Fliuch an oidhche, hu il oro
Is gum b'fhuair i, o hi i ibh o
Ach thug Clann Neill, hu il oro
Druim a' chuain orr', boch oirinn o.

WET AND BITTER THE NIGHT

I heard a tale, which sore disturbed me
That Clan Neil have taken again
to the seas.

Though wet and bitter the night
Clan Neil have put to sea
Many's the black rocky shore
they've raided.

They of the high sails
and of the fleet ships.
Men of the green and scarlet banners.

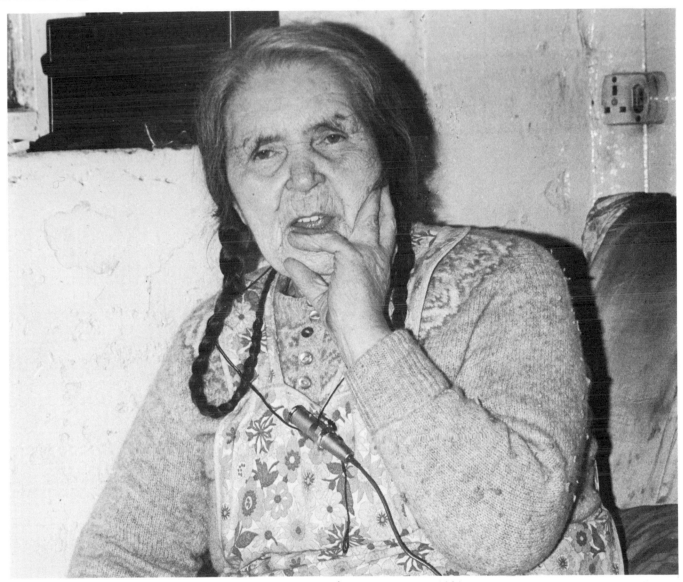

Nan McKinnon at home in Vatersay, 1981.

the better of him just let me carry on.' Anyway, they started fighting and the Bauch was getting the better of McNeill, so Gille Dubh went to his aid to help him and he killed the Bauch Sealltainneach. When McNeill saw that the Bauch was dead, he ordered all the cattle and sheep in Shetland to be raided and taken with them. But Gille Dubh Thangasdail turned on McNeill. 'No,' he says, 'it was I that did this and not you. It was I that killed the Bauch Sealltainneach and I've more right than you to the plunder and if you don't go to your birlin [boat] as fast as your legs can carry you, I'll do the very same to you.' So McNeill had to leave everything to Gille Dubh. The cattle and sheep were returned to their places in Shetland and Gille Dubh got the Bauch Sealltainneach's daughter and married her. He built a castle in Scalloway in Shetland and it still stands—well, the remains of it— and it's the very same shape as Castle Kisimul."

Another of the most notable characters to survive in the oral tradition is 'Marion of the Heads', a fifteenth-century wife of one of the McNeills of Barra. She herself was from Coll but she gained notoriety in Barra as Marion of the Heads after the death of the chief when she ruled during the minority of their son. She had the habit of decapitating those she took a dislike to, including her two stepsons who might have had a better claim to the chiefship than her son. She had a servant behead these boys and then she took the heads herself down to the cemetery, washed them in the well and gave them Christian burial there. Nan McKinnon relates the strange story of how one of her victim's sons wrought uncanny revenge on Marion's servant, who was responsible for carrying out her series of executions.

Nan McKinnon:
"The father went to where the heads of his sons were, so as to bury them at Borve. He carried them in a cradle and when he was coming along and taking a short-cut across a place called Cliff, one of the heads spoke and said 'Father, you'll go to the island of Fuday and there's a young woman there that I ought to have married and she's bearing my child. Go and bring her home with you and look

A Bhradag Dubh

Very Free

A' Bhradag Dubh | O hi o hu | A bhrist na glas-an | A ho ri

ho ho a o oh hi uu ri ho | Fal u a ho | Ho hi ho u.

Ge de bh'agaibh riamh	Barraidh bheag	C'aite na dh'fhag thu	Is Gilleoghnan
O hi o hu	O hi o hu	O hi o hu	O hi o hu
Ach Barraidh bheag,	Chrian dhubh chlachach	Niall a' Chaisteil	Mor an gaisgeach
A ho ri ho . . .	A ho ri ho . . .	A ho ri ho . . .	A ho ri ho . . .

Bheireadh a fion	Air ghaol uisge	'Sa chuireadh cruidhean
O hi o hu	O hi o hu	O hi o hu
Dha chuid eachaibh	Loin a sheachnadh	Oir fo'n casan
A ho ri ho . . .	A ho ri ho . . .	A ho ri ho . . .

THE BLACK BESOM

(Uist Woman) *You Black Besom
What have you McNeills ever had
but your little Barra–wee,
bare, black, stony Barra.*

(Barra Woman) *What we have had, the
likes of you could never
aspire to
Neil of the Castle
Neil Frasach
the warrior, great Gillionan
who shod his steeds with gold
and gave them such wine to drink
that they disdained to touch water.*

after her well and she'll bear a son and he'll seek my revenge.'

"So the poor father went for the girl and took her home, looked after her and it came to pass that she had the son as was foretold. He grew up and when he was twelve years of age it happened on a hot day in summer that they were shearing sheep in Borve and this young boy was walking round they that were shearing sheep. One of the men asked him, 'Now, my boy, just you take that cuman [a water bucket] and bring me a drink from the well.' The boy took the cuman, filled it with water and when he was coming back he let it fall on a rock and broke it to bits. He went back to the man that asked for the drink and he says, 'Oh, I'm so sorry, I've broken the cuman.' 'Oh,' the man said, 'my boy, don't cry, I'll drink from the well.' And he went and the boy followed him and when he bent down, bent his head down to get his drink, the boy took a sword from the sleeve of his coat, hit him at the back of the head and left his head in the well. 'Now,' he says, 'that's what you've done to my father.' Whether it was instinctive or whether the boy was told about it remains a mystery, but it did happen."

Marion herself met her fate in 1540 when the Barra people apparently revolted against her. She had one last request, that she be buried not in Barra but in Coll. On the day, however, that the party set out with her body to Coll, a northerly gale blew up and she was buried off Vatersay at Capal Mor Nan Ceann, the chapel of the heads, outside the chapel, and standing upright facing Coll.

Despite the fact that almost the entire population of Barra were of Clan Neil, some families of different clans were to be found, for example McKinnons, who came from Elgol in Skye in the sixteenth century as grazing constables to McNeill of Barra. Perhaps the most interesting story, however, is that of how the first McPhees came to Barra, and ultimately the island of Mingulay.

Nan McKinnon:
"The McPhees of Colonsay, the first one that arrived in Barra was a Kenneth McPhee and that was at the time when all the people of Eigg were burned to death in St Francis cave by McLeod of Dunvegan. Kenneth McPhee who was married to McDonald of Eigg's daughter was the only one to escape. They had a baby son three or four months old and McPhee went to his own home after he escaped from the cave, wrapped the baby in a blanket and took it to his own boat. He didn't care where he went to, as long as he'd get away from the horrors of Eigg. He landed in Barra, built a sort of house for himself and married again.

"Now one day years later, McNeill of Barra was wondering why he wasn't seeing anyone coming from the island of Mingulay [with his rent]. He sent a boat with a crew over to the island and one of the young men that was in the crew was the baby that was brought from Eigg by his father. He was seventeen years of age by this time and when they landed over at Mingulay one of the older men said, 'Just go up and see what's doing.' They didn't see anyone, there was no sign of life, and he went up to all the houses and found they were all dead. Some of them had pots on the fire, some of them were lyin' on the floor, some of them were in their beds. And och, he rushed down and when he was gettin' near the beach he called at the pitch of his voice, 'Oh, God,' he cried, 'they're all dead!'

"The men in the boat said, 'Well, is there anything the matter with them? If it's any disease or a plague or anything, you've got your stomach full of it and you'd better stay along with them,' and they pushed their boat away and left the poor boy cryin' there on the rocks. So he stayed there till nightfall and it got dark. He went right round the island, right round to the south of Mingulay and built a shelter for himself. Fortunately he had a pocket knife and he used to kill the sheep, and it's said that he lived mostly on the fat of the sheep. He was there for six weeks alone and he used to climb to the top of the hill—it's called McPhee's hill to this day—to see if any boat was coming. No, he wasn't seeing any and he was there for six whole weeks, but then his father was wondering what had happened. He went down to McNeill and said, 'I was wondering what happened to my son, he was one of the crew.' McNeill never answered him and Kenneth McPhee knew that there was something he didn't want to tell. 'Now,' he says, 'if you don't tell me what happened to my son the lowest stone of your house will be the highest of it. You'll suffer for it.' So McNeill said, 'Well, Kenneth, your son was left over in Mingulay the day they were over to see what was wrong with the Mingulay people. Seeing it's happened just you pick your own men,' he says, 'and go to Mingulay and it'll be yours as long as any of your family lives.'

"And McPhee picked his own men, went to Mingulay, and they had it free of rent till such time as Colonel Gordon bought Barra in the nineteenth century and made them pay rent."

As a clan, the McNeills of Barra did not participate in the disastrous rebellion of 1745. Prudence determined the action of most of the Highland chiefs on that occasion. The repercussions, however, were to be great for Gaeldom as a whole, and not just the small minority of clans who had participated in the Rebellion. The real significance of Culloden was that it was the prelude to a massive government assault on the political, social and economic structure of the Highlands. The whole weight of government was employed to dissolve every tie between chief and clan and to abolish all distinction between Highland and Lowland Scot. Government legislation alone, however, could never have achieved this, and what was to be ultimately responsible for the end of the clan

Eoligary House, built c. 1790. Residence of Colonel Roderick McNeill, the 40th Chief.

system was summed up by A. J. Youngson as 'contact with and acceptance of the economic usages and ambitions of commercial and industrial capitalism of the Lowlands'.

For the majority of clan chiefs long accustomed to moving in the cultural spheres of both Gaeldom and Lowland society, the transition from a patriarchal figure to a capitalist landlord was a fairly easy one. In this respect the '45 Rebellion merely acted as a catalyst to accelerate modernising tendencies already at work in the Highlands. The overriding priority in estate management became commercial profit as against the number of able-bodied men on the clan lands. This transformation took place in Barra as elsewhere and ended the role of the McNeill towards his clan as it had been known. The first group to feel the winds of change were the tacksmen or middle class of the old clan system. There was little place for them in the new order and rather than succumb to transforming to business like farmers, most chose voluntary emigration. This was to prove one of the great catastrophies of Gaeldom in that it deprived the Highlands of its natural middle class and the ordinary people of their natural leadership. There was much 'voluntary' emigration in Barra between 1760 and 1790. Colonel Roderick McNeill wrote in 1790 'deploring the loss of so many decent people', but he was to be the last proprietor of Barra to express regret at the emigration of his tenants. Perhaps due to its relative isolation and the close-knit nature of the community, Barra was later in manifesting the deterioration in relationship between chief and clansmen, but in 1822 the last chief of the McNeills in the direct line, General Roderick McNeill, succeeded his father.

Nan McKinnon:

"It was prophesied centuries before that it would be Ruaraidh, the seventh Ruaraidh, that would lose Barra, and it came to pass that it was the seventh Ruaraidh who had to sell Barra. He started glassworks down at North Bay, went bankrupt and had to sell Barra to pay his debts."

Eoligary House with demolition squad, 1975.

Thatched houses, Barra, c 1900.

As in all the seaboard areas in the Highlands, the kelp industry became very important in Barra in the late eighteenth century, early nineteenth century. Kelp was an extremely lucrative activity for the clan chiefs given that in 1794, tenants received on average £2.5/- a ton, while the chiefs sold it at anything from £10 to £22 a ton. Rents were also raised during this period and thus the chiefs scored a double bonus. By 1814, however, the price for kelp began to fall and General Roderick McNeill came into kelp on a falling market. The alkali works he built at North Bay between 1830 and 1833 were a financial disaster. Hard pressed financially to raise cash, McNeill divided every croft in Barra in two, charged the same rent and thus doubled the apparent value of his property. General McNeill's memory has probably benefitted from comparison with his successor as proprietor, Colonel Gordon of Cluny. The following letter, however, written in London in July 1825 to the Rev. Angus McDonald, at a time when McNeill was frantically trying to organise his commercial enterprises in Barra, is a sad testimony to the last chief of McNeills in the direct line.

"I think it but fair candidly to tell you that the conduct and tone of the good people of Barra, whom every day's experience teaches me cannot be depended upon from their fickleness, idleness and stiff necked prejudice, has produced in my mind a decided revolution. Every man, my good sir, has a right to do the best he can for himself in his own affairs — if one set of servants won't do, the master must try others. I cannot afford the slow operation of waiting till John or Thomas or Hamish are pleased to be convinced that McNeill after all was right and could not have meant to cheat and ruin them. No, Mr Angus, I see my way sufficiently clear before me, but if I am to ensure myself an ample harvest, I must have fishers and kelpers who will cheerfully do my bidding. In the name of common sense abandon all idea of condescensions on my part to your spoilt children. Pray do not ask me as my resolve is not to be shaken. So if you mean to keep your flock together, look to it. I can easily fill up the vacancies. Say to the fishermen that if they do not within 8 and 40 hours after this proclamation bend their energies to the daily prosecution of their calling as fishermen, I shall turn every man of them off the island were they steeped to the ears in debt. Say to those who are about to emigrate I sincerely wish them well through it and assure those who have signed and repented that their repentance comes too late. So help me God they shall go at all events from my property, every man, woman and child."

McNeill, however, went bankrupt and Barra's vastly increased population of some 2,300 were unemployed and quite unable to pay the inflated rents McNeill had imposed during the kelp boom. Barra was put in the hands of creditors and was bought for £42,000 in 1839 by a speculator called Menzies. In 1840 Menzies put it up for sale at Paxton's Coffee House in Inverness where it was purchased for only £38,000 by Gordon of Cluny. Thus, after forty generations of McNeills of Barra it had been sold twice in one year. Colonel Gordon was to be responsible for some of the most barbaric evictions in the Highlands during the last century.

Nan McKinnon:

"They just lived on the rocks in Barra and there's an old man lived beside us, he was our neighbour where I was brought up and he used to tell us that his father, who was born down in Uig there at the jetty, had to flee at such short notice that they took the roof off the house in the morning and slept under the same roof that night in another place.

"Gordon evicted the crofters from the whole island of Vatersay, and from the adjacent islands, and from Tangeval—they were evicted from all those places."

The onset of the potato famine in 1845-46 blasted the Barra people's last hopes of retaining life upon their small unproductive patches. By 1847 the critical proportions of the famine in Barra came to the attention of the authorities. Colonel Gordon had provided some employment on roadworks but in August 1846 these projects had been abandoned and the workers dismissed. Informed by his factor that at least 8,000 bolls of meal would be required to prevent widespread destitution, Gordon, who lived in Aberdeenshire, made arrangements to 'send 900 Bolls'.

By January 1843 none of these had arrived in Barra and the island was quoted as the most wretched of all Highland estates. Colonel Gordon hit upon a somewhat novel solution to the problem and solicited Government through the Home Secretary to purchase Barra for a penal colony. Fortunately he was told 'it would not suit'.

In the three years between 1848 and 1851 Gordon was responsible for the transportation to Canada of some 2,715 people from his estates in Barra and South Uist.

The coming of the Crofters Commission in 1883 marked the turn of the tide in the fortunes of the Barra people, as elsewhere in the Highlands. Slowly but surely the economic conditions of the island began to improve but there still remained an acute shortage of land due to the letting of large tracts of land to outside farmers. On the 8th of September 1900, the farm of Northbay, one of the largest on the island, was illegally occupied and others quickly followed the same fate. The most daring series of raids was carried out by men from the island of Mingulay who successfully established their community on Vatersay between 1900 and 1908.

By the turn of the century then, the lot of the Barra people, as elsewhere, had improved greatly; most importantly the crofter now had security of tenure.

Archie McDonald:

"Barra was thriving very well in the early part of the century, fishing was great, there was a lot of

The Herring Boom, Castlebay, c. 1910.

Peat carriers and Barra ponies, c. 1915.

herring, with whitefishing in the winter, and the seafaring boys were away at sea and doing well till that mass defeat of the '14 war came and struck. Families were scattered all over. In Barra most joined the Royal Navy and a lot was in the Merchant Service too, that never came back. After all that the First World War boys were going to come home, they told them they would come back to a land flowing with milk and honey, aye, that was the show till the Depression of the early 'twenties struck. All the beautiful herring boats were drawn up, there was no market for herring and no market for fish. The same thing happened with cattle and sheep and everything went down, and the Merchant Navy also went down at that time. That's what happened really till the next boost came and the next war hit us again. The last war saw a big difference in Barra, in all the islands I think, but I think it was noticed more in the smaller islands. A lot of old people was left and the younger people moved away. It was sad. It was depopulation in a way but in the last few years there's been a halt—maybe things are changing."

Today the population of Barra appears to have stabilised, and the drain of young people away from the island halted to some degree. The traditional means of livelihood—crofting, fishing, the sea, are still the backbone of the community. Recent co-operative ventures have been fairly successful as has the establishment of a fish processing plant, but for the young people, employment in oil-related industries has probably been of greatest importance in job terms.

One thousand years after the arrival of Niall of the Castle in Barra, McNeill is still the predominant name in the island and the majority of the local population are still Gaelic speaking. Clan McNeill, however, have scattered to all corners of the globe, well illustrated by the fact that the present chief is an American. Wherever the McNeills were to go, identity was never surrendered easily.

D. J. McLean:
"When the clearances was on they left. Some of them landed in Cape Breton and they put up their own places there and called it Barra Glen and there was 400 McNeills in it."

During the later eighteenth and nineteenth centuries the Highland clan was to become popular amongst romantics and the notion of the 'braw John Heilan' man' decked in his clan tartan, tramping the glen, was born. It was an image exploited by the military establishment who would successfully channel the energies of the clan regiments against 'Britannia's' enemies. The romantic image of the Highland clan has been an enduring one, perpetuated by advertising, the media and the popularity of 'tartan and heather' societies. It is indeed fortunate that people like Nan McKinnon can still remind us of the depth of Gaelic oral tradition, and provide us with something approaching a truer impression of the clan period.
BILLY ROSS

SCOTLAND
SOBER AND FREE
The Temperance Movement 1829 ~ 1979

People's Palace Museum
Glasgow Green
3 October 1979 ~ 31 January 1980
10 am ~ 5 pm daily, 2 pm ~ 5 pm Sundays
Admission free

Whisky's Awa'?

In Scotland an estimated 75,000-112,000 people over the age of fifteen have what is termed 'a drink problem'. Alcohol abuse, according to bodies such as the Scottish Council on Alcoholism, is the cause of many health and social problems, and the contemporary advertising campaign of the Scottish Health Education Unit, which is designed to either shame or scare Scots into drinking less, is widely known.

Similar but voluntary efforts of past generations to cope with excessive drinking in 'whisky-injured Scotland' have been all but forgotten. Temperance and teetotalist principles are now out of favour, badly understood and often confused with Gradgrind Calvinism and Scottish sabbatarianism. Few people realise the social impact which the temperance movement had in Scotland, or the cultural enrichment which it brought to people living in squalor, misery and hopelessness. Indeed, the essence and humour of the movement can be best heard from oral sources, which bring to life the dry and often passionless reports of the various temperance societies.

Temperance was introduced into Scotland in 1829 by John Dunlop (1789-1868), a philanthropic lawyer from Greenock. The cause was taken up and the message spread by William Collins, the Glasgow printer, who not only gave it considerable personal and financial backing, but put his press into its service. Their ideas were considered at best absurd, and at worst insidious, by a nation which prided itself on its conviviality. When Chartists and radicals in the early 1830s embraced teetotal principles wholeheartedly, many industrialists and established church ministers felt threatened. Workmen who compared their enslavement to drink with the enslavement imposed by their employers were considered a menace, and those who took to preaching against drink were effectively usurping the authority of the church. Radicalism and temperance were closely associated for over a century, Conservative interests resting naturally with those of the brewers and distillers.

Although the temperance movement cannot be described as a homogeneous or unified movement, neither can it be seen in terms of a minority or sectarian interest. From small beginnings, it grew to touch upon almost every facet of life in Scotland. By the turn of the century, the sum total of temperance effort had resulted in a radical change in attitude towards excessive drinking. The 'convivial topers' of an earlier age were now looked upon as irresponsible drunkards, and had the Scottish M.P.s been left to their own devices, temperance legislation in Scotland would have

The brothers who founded the Independent Order of Good Templars in Scotland, 1869 (wearing the coveted regalia).

been much more extensive than the ineffectual Temperance (Scotland) Act of 1913.

Temperance was a driving force in both local and national politics. Local politicians fought the loose licensing laws of the time, while at a national level, M.P.s pressed for legislation. It was the candidate of the Scottish Prohibition Party, Edwin Scrymgeour (1866-1947) who unseated Churchill in Dundee in 1922, and the Scottish Independent Labour Party members who accompanied him to Parliament in that year were likewise supporters of either temperance or prohibition. Those involved in left-wing politics who 'took a drink' were frowned upon, and a co-operative society which did not practise temperance principles could not become a member of the great Scottish Co-operative Wholesale Society.

Temperance principles came to be accepted by all churches. Every Presbyterian church had its Band of Hope, while the Catholic churches had their own temperance societies, established first by Father Mathew in the 1840s.

Ultimately, the various temperance organisations such as the Good Templars, Rechabites and Sons of Temperance and the bodies of the left—the I.L.P., Clarion Scouters and Co-operative societies—had managed to provide for their members an alternative, drink-free society. There were public houses and other places of entertainment without alcohol fed by a flourishing soft drinks industry; concerts of temperance songs sung by temperance choirs in temperance halls; coffee houses and tea rooms; temperance hotels; teetotal pleasure steamers; financial benefits in the form of lower insurance premiums. Indeed, one could go from the cradle to the grave, without stepping outside the movement.

Mrs Kerr:
"There were five generations of us in Good Templary. I was carried in to the Order, and I came right up through the Order. My mother was a singer, and my aunts were singers, and in the Good Templars they were known as the Gibson Sisters. It was just natural for me to carry on there."

Robert McKechnie:
"We had at that time a Cradle Roll. So more or less your name was added almost as soon as you were born. But I took a very active part in the Juvenile Lodge, from say five years old onwards and at that time, all the children around our area were members of the Juvenile Lodge. When we reached the age of roughly fourteen, we were transferred into what we looked upon as the 'big' lodge."

The problem of child drunkenness should not be underestimated. Until 1913, children could collect drink from the pubs for their parents in jugs and mugs.

James Myatt:
"At that time, when we went up for a pint of beer and it was filled up, they used to let you suck the froth. If a boy was going for beer for his father, you said 'Gaun up for beer, Wullie? Aye right, I'll come with ye'—so we went up and had a suck at the froth of the beer."

The Bands of Hope therefore made tremendous efforts to educate children against alcohol. Besides this, they were a source of free entertainment and great enjoyment.

Jan Goudie:
"It was really quite something. I don't remember what age I was but in your young days your entertainment and places to go to were more or less organised by churches, and one of them was called Paddy Black's Mission. And you used to go in there, and you got handed a big enamel mug. And if there was a crowd, you all got packed tight in. And they gave you a bag of buns going in. There would be someone would give you a talk you know—a religious talk, and about the slides you were going to see.

"You were always in a bit of a quandary as to what to do. In the one hand you had a bag of buns, and then they'd come round with scalding hot tea. And you'd this mug of tea, and if you laid it down, it got kicked over. If you put your buns down, they disappeared. So you held on to your tea, kept your buns in your lap, started eating your buns, and you got drier and drier. People were joggling you, it was a free-for-all, and the noise! I can still remember it—it was unbelievable!

"Quite often you couldn't finish your buns, or you were going to keep one to take home. If you thought the slides were lousy, you started throwing the buns.

"But the reason why most of the kids went to the Band of Hope was that unless you went to the Band of Hope or the Sunday School, you couldn't get to Paddy Black's Trip. And that was something. The carters round about, like Robb in Commerce Street, Lurdies, all these people, used to decorate their carts, either put forms on them or layers of straw, and all the kids could sit on them. The horses were beautifully groomed, with all their fancy decorations and plumes, and what have you. And all the local bands—the pipe band, the B.B. Bugle Band, all the bands interspersed in this very very long procession—there must have been about sixty or seventy carts. And you either went to Bellahouston Park or Pollok Estate—one of these places. The whole of Glasgow used to turn out to watch this trip going away."

Mrs Kerr:
"Outings and trips, and they celebrated different nights—Halloween nights, and my mother had always a big dumpling on for Halloween nights and there was the guisers, all dressed up. Prizes went for the best-dressed guiser. Every occasion, Christmas and all those occasions."

The Drunkard's Raggit Wean.

WORDS BY PAUL ROOKFORD.

MUSIC BY THE KIND PERMISSION OF MESSRS D. SWAN & CO.,
70 Buchanan Street,
Of whom Copies of the Tune, with Piano-Forte accompaniment, may be had.

With Feeling.

A wee bit rag-git lad-die gangs wan'-ren thro' the street, Wad-in' mang the snaw wi' his

wee hack-it feet, Shiv'-rin' i' the cauld blast, greet-in' wi' the pain, Wha's the puir wee

cal-lan'? he's a drunkard's rag-git wean. He stans at il-ka door, and he keeks wi' wist-fu' e'e, To

see the crowd around the fire, a' laugh-in' loud wi' glee; But he daur-na ven-ture ben, tho' his

heart be e'er sae fain, For he man-na play wi' i-ther bairns, the drunk-ard's rag-git wean.

Oh see the wee bit bairnie, his heart is unco fou,
The sleet is blawin' cauld, and he's dreepit through and through;
He's speerin' for his mither, an' he wun'ers whar she's gane;
But oh! his mither she forgets her puir wee raggit wean.
He kens na faither's luve, an' he kens na mither's care,
To soothe his wee bit sorrows, or kame his tautit hair,
To kiss him when he waukens, or smooth his bed at e'en,
An' oh! he fears his father's face, the drunkard's raggit wean.

Oh pity the wee laddie, sae guileless an' sae young,
The oath that lea's the father's lip 'ill settle on his tongue;
An' sinfu' words his mither speaks his infant lips 'ill stain,
For oh there's nane to guide the bairn, the drunkard's raggit wean!
Then surely we micht try an' turn that sinfu' mither's heart,
An' try to get his father to act a father's part,
An' mak them lea' the drunkard's cup, an' never taste again,
An' cherish wi' a parent's care their puir wee raggit wean.

Just Published, Price One Penny,

THE CRYSTAL FOUNT SONG BOOK,

Containing nearly One Hundred TEMPERANCE SONGS, &c., several of which are by
the author of ' The Drunkard's Raggit Wean.'

GLASGOW:

W. NIVEN, 71 EGLINTON STREET; SCOTTISH TEMPERANCE LEAGUE, 108 HOPE STREET.
LONDON: W. TWEEDIE, 337 STRAND. EDINBURGH: J. DICKSON, 10½ NICOLSON STREET.

S. AND T. DUNN,]   [PRINTERS, GLASGOW.

Temperance song. Inset illustration by George Cruickshank, from a Scottish Society for Suppressing Drunkenness publication, 1852.

Temperance organisations often brought some colour and excitement into the lives of children, and the right to wear regalia, which accompanied membership of the Good Templars, Rechabites and Sons of Scotland was an added bonus.

Martin Robertson:

"One thing I will always remember was the fact that when I was initiated into the juvenile branch of Good Templary, officers had to wear their regalia round their neck. I envied them that right from the start and I wasn't satisfied until after about a year in the Order I was promoted to holding an office. The regalia which the officers of the Lodge wore was a purple collar, with the words 'IOGT' on one side and our motto, 'Faith, Hope and Charity', on the other. Now as youngsters we were all keen to wear one of those regalias."

The magic lantern show, which was the staple entertainment of the Band of Hope, often excited the imagination.

J. B. Owens:

"I was a regular attender at the Gairbraid Church Band of Hope in Burnhouse Street, Maryhill. I have never failed to remember some of the scenes, particularly of sea-coasts or lighthouses, and when I have been, in the course of my business life, to places like Peterhead and Fraserburgh, and also into Banff and Buckie, where some of the glorious scenes of setting suns are to be observed, I've always remembered that the first time I had witnessed such glorious scenes was at the Band of Hope, through some of the slides that those good people tried to show us. Because they lifted us completely from what was a working-class life—none of us had ever seen the sea."

Jan Goudie:

"Two slides I can distinctly remember. One of the head of Christ with the crown of thorns, all in lurid, vivid colours. And another slide was a photograph of a pub door with all the adverts for spirits and beers, and three wee waifs, different sizes, standing outside the door. There was a talk about that, on the evils of alcohol, and what it did to the poor mother and the children, and the next slide had a song on it—something like 'Father dear father come home'—inferring that the kids were starving and all the rest of it."

Mr Kerr:

"When I was very young, I joined the Band of Hope in our church in Hamilton. They had marvellous meetings. I always remember one in particular, a Mr Gibb gave a lecture and he had alcohol with him. He was giving examples of the uses of alcohol. He says, 'You know, away up in Alaska, they don't have fires as such. They don't have fires with coal or wood, or anything like that

Pledge card of J. B. Owens.

because there is no wood or coal.' So he says, 'They use alcohol,' and he says, 'I'll let you see how it's done.' And he poured the alcohol into a receptacle, and put a match to it, and it went in flames. He says, 'This is the use of alcohol. It's the only good use of alcohol—to get a wee bit heat.' So this was the lecture we had in the Band of Hope."

William Brown:

"It was a year or two before the First War, and this American lawyer—his name was Tennyson Smith—he seemed to be carrying on campaigns on temperance in different places. He came to Motherwell, and was there a fortnight, with a meeting every night, and it climaxed in what he called 'A Trial of Alcohol'. Now on the Town Hall platform they had set up a sort of mock court with a dock, and a judge's place and so on, and there was a judge, jury, two counsel—and a bottle of whisky in the dock. The whole thing was overseen for legal purposes by the Town Clerk of Motherwell at that time, a Mr Burns. Now when the trial started of course, it was just a case of saying a few words from each counsel, and then they brought in their witnesses. Tennyson Smith's witnesses were, of course, very vehement against drink. The other chap, the defender, had only a few witnesses, but one of them was a local doctor who testified as to the medicinal value of spirits. But after the two counsels had made their closing speeches, the result was inevitable—guilty—and the judge pronounced sentence of death on the bottle of alcohol.

Somebody brought in a basin or a pail with a hammer, and they smashed the bottle into this pail. And that was the whole thing finished. It was quite a thrilling night for Motherwell because at that time we didn't have the cinemas as much as we have now, and of course there was no TV and no radio."

Band of Hope leaders made up poems to try to impress upon children the addictive qualities of drink. The following is from Mrs Sykes' vast repertoire.

Bessie Sykes:

A little grey mouse one fine summer's day,
Said to his mother, "I'm going away.
I'm tired of this place, it is not very gay,
And I've made up my mind not to stay here alway."
His mother was sad, and heaved a great sigh,
And said "My dear son, very sorry am I.
But if you must go, one thing I must say,
If you're once in a mousetrap, you'll ne'er get away!"
"All right," said the mouse, so plump and so grey,
As in the bright sunshine he trotted away;
And smiled, as he thought of his mother's advice,
Though she was the oldest and wisest of mice.
As he went on his journey such strange things he met,
But he said to himself, "I've not seen a trap yet,
And I'll not be afraid, though mother did say,
'If you're once in a mousetrap, you'll ne'er get away'."
Soon mousey grew hungry and longed for some food,
"Oh," he cried, "I can smell something good;
'Tis cheese! Toasted cheese—I know very well!"
And he ran to the spot from whence came the sweet smell.
"A dear little house! Oh can it be real?
Just the place for a mouse to have a good meal.

The door is just open—I don't mean to stay."
But the door held him fast—he could not get away.
To remember his mother's advice was too late,
And bitterly now did he moan his sad fate.
His mother and home he saw never more,
Just because he once entered that fatal trap door.
My tale has a moral, though simple 'tis true,
The drink is the mousetrap, the grey mouse is you;
The drink is the bait, a delusion and snare,
And you will be caught, if you do not take care.

Mr Kerr:

"Our minister took the Band of Hope you know. He used to come in, and the first thing he'd say 'How many letters is the Pledge?' Of course he only wanted the Pledge—P-L-E-D-G-E—six letters. And this was always the wee things that started things away. And then every week you said the Pledge. Every week.

I promise here by Grace Divine,
To take no spirits, ale or wine;
Nor will I buy nor sell nor give,
Strong drink to others while I live.
For my own good this pledge I take,
And also for my neighbour's sake;
And this my strong resolve will be,
No drink, no drink, no drink for me."

Adults often found that signing the pledge was of great help in their attempts to break free of drink addiction, and many of the Gospel Missions tried to help them.

James Myatt worked in the Tolbooth Mission at Glasgow Cross in the early 1920s:

Women queueing to enter the Tent Hall, c. 1890.

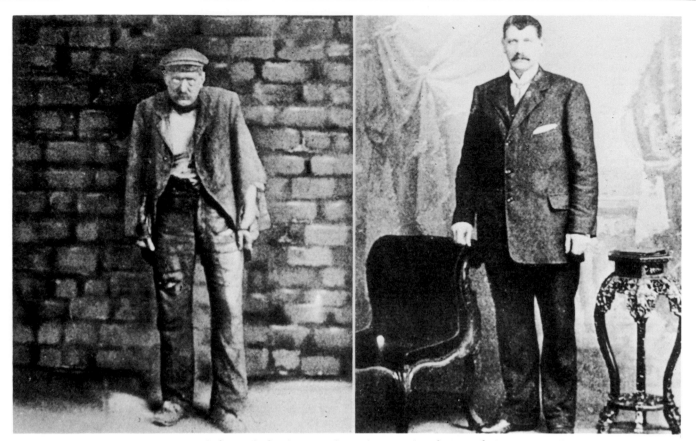

Jimmy Byars, before and after (1910 and 1912)–a Trophy of Grace of the Tent Hall.

"They would take a notion and go to the Tolbooth and sign the pledge at the Tolbooth. 'I promise to abstain from liquor, alcohol in any shape or form', and the funny bit was, when they signed that, they kep it! They'd keep it maybe for a month, two month, three month, longer, just by signing that pledge. And that was an excuse—you could hear a man say 'C'mon, have a pint, Wullie.' 'Naw—I've signed the pledge, I've signed the pledge.' That was all right—nobody pressed them when they said they'd signed the pledge. They were tryin', they were doin' their best, to get better conditions, to make better conditions for themselves.

"The Tolbooth Mission held gospel tea meetings and, periodically, Muffler Meetings. You had to be in a better class—even although I was unemployed I had to wear a collar and tie because I was a member o' the mission. For the Muffler Meetings the chairman and everybody put on a muffler, to invite the people, to encourage the people, wearin' mufflers to come into the meetin'. And they had a tea meetin' and maybe gave them a pie, cakes or something like that. And the whole idea was to preach to them, try and get them to sober up and become members of the Tolbooth—all the missions did that."

Such mission halls were popular throughout Scotland, and played an important part in the religious education of working-class people, succeeding where the established churches had failed dismally. In Glasgow, mission work was co-ordinated by the Glasgow United Evangelical Association, established in 1874 in the wake of the triumphant visit of Moody and Sankey. The G.U.E.A.'s best-known work was done in the Tent Hall in Steel Street, off Saltmarket. The mission had its origins in a gospel tent on Glasgow Green, where open-air meetings reached thousands who had never been inside a church, and from 1875 to 1979 it specialised in the care and reclamation of drunkards.

Mrs Sykes:

"Jimmy Byars was one who got converted at the Tent Hall, and many were in the same boat at that. And I've a feeling it was Jimmy Byars who said he believed in miracles—that the Lord could do wonderful things. Jesus turned water into wine—well, the Lord turned beer into furniture for him. And there were people who used to be all right, and their downfall was drink and they started again by getting converted in the Free Breakfast and took up life again and became real trophies.

"There used to be a lady—her name was Mrs Dunbar—in the Tent Hall who looked after that section of the work—women and girls who were outcasts from society. Maybe drink was their downfall, or some other thing. And they would come in, and she would look after them. She would clothe them if they needed clothing, feed them if they needed feeding, all in connection with the Tent Hall work. And she would try and get them a new start in life and help them on the way."

Whisky's Awa'

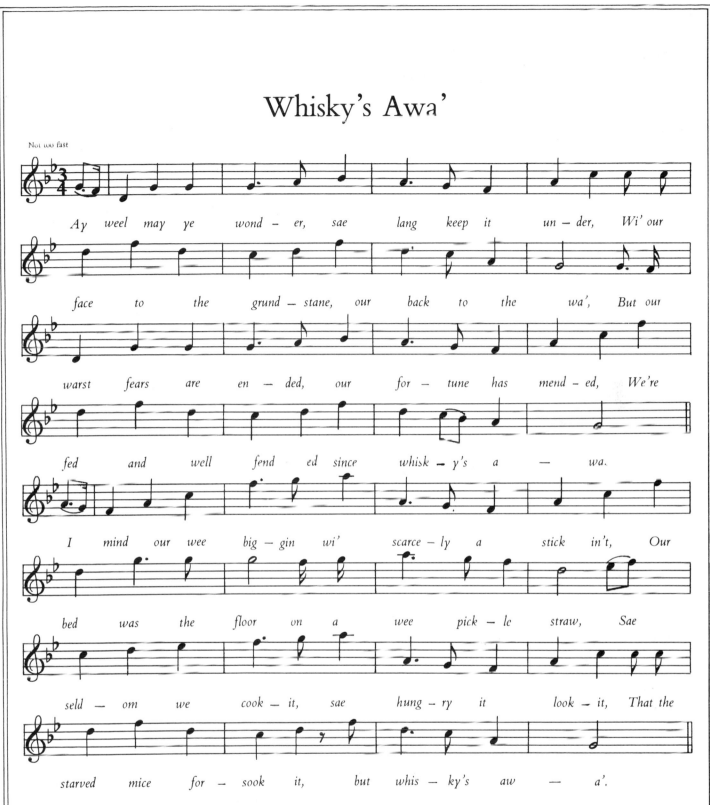

Not too fast

Ay weel may ye wond — er, sae lang keep it un — der, Wi' our
face to the grund — stane, our back to the wa', But our
warst fears are en — ded, our for — tune has mend — ed, We're
fed and well fend ed since whisk — y's a — wa.
I mind our wee big — gin wi' scarce — ly a stick in't, Our
bed was the floor on a wee pick — le straw, Sae
seld — om we cook — it, sae hung — ry it look — it, That the
starved mice for — sook it, but whis — ky's aw — a'.

See noo, whit a change—we've a weel-stockit girnel—
Abundance o' bannocks, wi' hams ane or twa;
Our fire it is cheery—sae dull ance and eerie—
Can shelter the weary—since whisky's awa.

Ye thoughtless, who rin on the rough road to ruin,
Come, join total abstinence!—join ane and a'!
For naething can mend ye, nae kind friend will fend ye—
Nae guid will attend ye, till whisky's awa!

Bessie and Seth Sykes were a Springburn couple who became known throughout Britain for their evangelical and temperance teachings. Their mission began on the streets of Glasgow during the General Strike.

Bessie Sykes:

"There was a lot of children and people couldn't get on holiday in the summer of 1926 for they had no money to do anything like that, and we got the idea to start these meetings, to gather the children together up at Alford Street, and the parents became just as interested. And we started in the summer of 1926 and went on for three years—every summer for three years. And at first, we wondered how they would go—we had a kind of handful at first, but it grew and grew all the time, until night after night we had quite a good following. It was amazing the people that gathered round, and where they came from.

"From Monday to Friday without fail we had the meetings. We carried this little organ, the organ was getting kind of done that we had. I used to say that it had asthma, bronchitis, it was developing consumption, and we were badly needing another organ. But, it was going to be difficult to get one—a portable organ. But here, before we knew anything about it, the children and the friends of the meeting, they gathered between them and got us another organ to take the place of the one that was on its last legs, and it was presented to us to carry on the work in those meetings. They all put

Mrs Bessie Sykes at her new organ, c. 1928. The organ is now in the People's Palace.

together and they put a wee plate on it saying it had been presented to us by the children and friends who attended the meetings."

Peter Donnelly:

"In those days, hundreds of children congregated round about the streets and played out in the open, because most of the houses were single ends, and room and kitchens, and there was nothing else for them to do but go out and play in the streets. And word would come round that Seth Sykes was coming. And he appeared in Gourlay Street—he used to walk up the centre of the street, and he wheeled a trolley with the organ on it, and all the kids following him from the further ends of Springburn.

"He used to hand out bills, and it said 'Mr and Mrs Seth Sykes, assisted by the Tiny Tots Trio' (that was the three kids—they sang gospel hymns, and Mrs Sykes played the organ).

"He never took any collections at his meeting—he was a tramway driver or conductor. The only time I ever knew him to take a collection was when he got the Salvation Army band to come up and add a bit more entertainment to it one night, and there was a big turnout for that. And as he mentioned himself, he never took collections, but he was taking one that night for 'the best band in Springburn'. Then he would have other nights that were kind of gala nights, when he would ask all the kids to wear paper hats."

Open-air meetings were a common feature of temperance work, and the speakers were sometimes subjected to harassment.

James Myatt:

"There were six Open Airs at Bridgeton Cross at that time, back in the 1920s. There was the Bethany Hall, the Christian Volunteers, the Salvation Army and the Cairter's Mission, the Mill Street Mission. And there was one in Muslin Street. They could all get crowds at that time. I was the Staff Sergeant of the Christian Volunteers, in charge of the Open Air, and there used to be crowds at each meeting. And what happened, the publican of Hillcoats' Pub, the man in charge, complained about the crowds obstructing his door. So he sent for the police and the police cleared the pavement a bit, but they couldn't put us too far out. Of course in those days there were no motor cars or anything, and we could spread out a bit into the street. So he complained, the police came—but it was the rule that you couldn't disturb a gospel meeting—that was the rule. But you could be asked to move on. So he asked them to move on and I was singing a song, later on, after he had spoken to us, and we asked the crowd to come out. And after he had spoken to us I was singing this hymn, 'Courage Go On'. And the last verse is 'When burdens oppress ye and trials cast down, Remember, remember there

Scrymgeour holding an open-air meeting, Albert Square, c. 1913.

waits you a crown'. And as I was singing, I looked up, and on the lintel of the door was 'J. Burdons, Licenced to sell wine and spirits and tobacco'. And it was such a coincidence—'Burdens oppress ye'—you know, that was what I was talking about—such a coincidence me singing 'Burdens oppress ye'— and he was trying to oppress us, telling us to keep out of the way!''

A Dundee Good Templar remembers the open-air meetings held by Edwin Scrymgeour, founder of the Scottish Prohibition Party.

Martin Robertson:
"About 1913, Ned started a series of open-air meetings in the Albert Square which was known as the Speakers' Corner in Dundee, where advocates not only of religion but all the different political parties and sometimes even hawkers, addressed big meetings on Sunday evenings. Now I can easily remember one occasion when I happened to be there, though I was quite a young man at the time, when a questioner in the audience threw up the question at Neddy—'Ned, you're fond of a smoke. If I promise to give up drinking, will you give up smoking?' Ned took him at his word, he says 'I'll

stop smokin' now.' And he took his pipe out of the top pocket of his jacket, turned round and threw the pipe away into the grounds of the Albert Institute. He says, 'That's me finished with smoking.' He says, 'I hope you'll come back next week,' he says, 'and let me know if you have stuck by your side of the bargain and stopped drinking.' "

The temperance movement was always an international movement, and there was a frequent exchange of ideas and personnel between Scotland, other European countries, the U.S.A., Canada, Australia and New Zealand. In 1908, for example, Scrymgeour's Scottish Prohibition Party sponsored a Scottish tour for Carrie Nation, the 'Bar Room Smasher' and a veteran of the Kansas Whisky Wars.

Carrie and her followers believed in direct action, and had smashed up saloons when public prayer failed to work. Describing herself as a 'hatcheteer', she always appeared on public platforms with a Bible in one hand and a hatchet in the other, and some of the small hatchet-shaped brooches distributed on her 1908 tour have survived.

Carrie Nation was a feminist; the pursuit of women's rights and the cause of temperance were often synonymous.

Carrie Nation poster.

Robert McKechnie:

"That's another thing as far as the Good Templar Order is concerned. It was the first organisation (1869) that allowed women to take part in its meetings. The women were entitled to the same rights and privileges as the men. And there were very few organisations at that time where women were permitted to take part. And a number of women of outstanding merit were in the Order in the early days. Here in Largs for instance, the first woman to be Provost of Largs was a Good Templar—Mrs Morris. She was superintendent of the juvenile work in Scotland for over twenty years. Another instance of training in the Good Templar movement which fitted people for social work/public work, and she became the first woman to be Provost here in Largs."

Both women and children suffered terribly because of male drinking habits, and the spectre of 'The Drunkard's Raggit Wean' was unfortunately all too real.

James Myatt:

"In the winter of 1916, she couldn't afford to buy me boots. And I was workin' deliverin' milk, for the dairy at the corner of Tylefield Street, in my bare feet, with snow. And I met this wee mongol boy—on coming home after delivering my milk this wee chap was sitting in the public house door, crying his heart out. And I says, 'Whit's wrong?' 'Ah canny walk am cauld, ah canny walk am cauld.' And I lifted him and put him on my back, put his two bare feet in my pockets of the jacket I had, and took him down to the house that way. And I had my bare feet.

"Up by the Templeton's Carpet Factory in Fordneuk Street there must have been a boiler or something underneath the pavement, for there was a square stone that was always dry in the snow, and it was always warm. We used to stand on that—I wasna the only boy y'know—we used to stand on that and heat wur feet."

Poor people drank to forget their pain and misery.

James Myatt:

"I was black leadin' the grate one day when this woman came to the door and oh, she was all excited. She says, 'Oh, will ye come, Jimmy?' she says, 'there's a man being buried opposite us and there's nobody there to say a prayer nor nothin'.' So I went along to this street off Dalmarnock Road; the van was outside or rather the cab—the paupers' cab, and this man was at the door, outside the close, and he said, 'Is it you that's doing this job?' I said, 'Yes.' He said, 'Well hurry up—I want away.' So I went up to this house—nothing, absolutely nothing. The only thing that was in the house was this coffin and two tripods, you know, and a big tall man with a military moustache, and a woman at each end. Both of them were drunk and they were sitting crying. I looked in the fireplace and it was only a fire made up wi' bricks. Well what could you do? I said a prayer, read a scripture, and then the man came up. He said, 'Give us a hand here, Mac.' So I gave him a hand to shift the coffin into the paupers' van. The paupers' cab was a cab with a square box hanging fixed at the bottom. You put the coffin in there and anybody that wanted to go to the cemetery could go into the cab but he shoved the man into this long box and away he went.

"People drank sometimes to get them out of their misery. If they got a few coppers in their hand they were up to the nearest pub and had a bit of conversation with people and that, and it passed their time and helped them to forget for a while.

And the Labour Party at that time were very worried about it too and that's a thing that amazes me today, the Labour Party were advocating teetotalism and all that for the worker. They said that the drink was a tool of the master to keep the people sodden wi' drink and they wouldn't think of their conditions and fight for better conditions. And the Labour Party was strongly against strong drink at that particular time."

Robert McKechnie:

"The founder of the Labour Party, Keir Hardie, was District Chief Templar of Ayr District Lodge, and it was there he made his first speech, in a Good Templar Lodge. Out of the west of Scotland particularly at that time, practically all your leading political Labour workers were Good Templars, or had been Good Templars, and were still total abstainers."

Harry McShane:

"You take the most of them that were councillors in those days. They were all teetotal. There was P. G. Stewart, the first Labour Lord Provost, and his brother. Teetotal PG. And Maxton was teetotal. All the Clydeside M.P.s till George Buchanan in his latter days was seen with a bottle of beer in his pocket. That was in his latter days. For most of his life he was teetotal."

Robert McKechnie:

"If you go back, you find that the trade union movement was very much indebted to the Good Templars for the presiding officers. They got their training in the Good Templar Order and then they went to trade union meetings and were able to get up and express themselves.

"Of course the Co-op in those days was a total abstinence movement. They didn't have any licences—liquor licences or anything of that nature. That's practically a modern trend as far as the Co-op is concerned."

In spite of the work done by the temperance movement, the drinking problem in Scotland is as bad, if not worse, than it was at the turn of the century.

James Myatt:

"Alcohol in those days seemed to have a different effect. Now they want to stab, they want to fight, they want to rape. In those days they wanted to *sing*. You always saw a drunk man singing. . . . It sort of cheered them up, the alcohol in those days. But not now—it seems to turn them into animals."

Temperance work lost all the ground it had gained for a variety of complex reasons—two World Wars, which introduced many to drinking, the unpopularity of prohibition in America, the poor quality of Scottish temperance legislation, the advent of other attractions for young people.

Martin Robertson:

"Unfortunately, two World Wars created a decline in the movement, mainly because the men who were called up in the Forces enjoyed or were persuaded by the NAAFI to start beer drinking. This led to them sticking to that in their everyday life, making the work of our Order doubly hard. Over the years, temperance, instead of being a byword in the country is now something of a backward step. Despite all other endeavours to attract new members, several things have come in the way. To mention but one thing, we had strong juvenile lodges until the advent, strange to relate, of rock and roll. Now it may seem strange to mention rock and roll, but believe me, we in our lodges knew what it meant. Our youngsters failed to attend our meetings because they were out practising their rock and roll.

"In this modern age, they think they're more sophisticated and if you mention temperance to many of them, they'll ask ye 'What is temperance?' There's also the fact that the membership of churches has deteriorated rapidly not only in Dundee but all over the country, with the result that ministers do not have the opportunity of advocating temperance. In fact I know in my own church, we were reduced to one temperance service per quarter. This I believe has now resulted in one temperance night in the year. The Church of Scotland which used to spend maybe a matter of one or two days on the question of temperance [during the General Assembly], now devote, I believe, only one afternoon in the whole week's session to advocating temperance, and again, it's attended mainly by women. Notable absentees being the ministers."

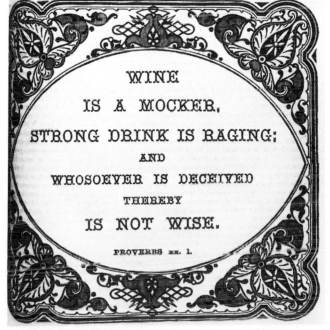

WINE
IS A MOCKER,
STRONG DRINK IS RAGING;
AND
WHOSOEVER IS DECEIVED
THEREBY
IS NOT WISE.

PROVERBS xx. 1.

Text from Scottish Temperance League publication.

ELSPETH KING

The '26

If anything else of historical importance happened in 1926 we could be forgiven for overlooking it, so much was that year dominated by the General Strike and miners' lock-out. Both events directly affected masses of ordinary working people, and both provided for many people the most intense, exhilarating, or depressing experiences of their lives.

This was the case, as elsewhere, in the East Fife coalfield. The coalfield extended eastward from Kirkcaldy along the Firth of Forth to Leven, and included mining towns or villages such as Wemyss —East Wemyss, West Wemyss, Coaltown of Wemyss—Buckhaven, Methil, Coaltown of Balgonie, and pits such as the Michael, the Wellesley, Muiredge, Lochhead, the Rosie, and Wellsgreen. The pits were owned by either of two private companies, the Fife Coal Company and the Wemyss Coal Company. The miners' county union in Fife had split in 1923, mainly over issues of internal democracy and leadership; and when the big events of 1926 unfolded there were still two rival unions in the county—the 'Old' Union, whose general secretary was the right-wing Labour M.P. William Adamson, and the more militant

Reform Union, whose secretary, Philip Hodge, had been expelled from the Independent Labour Party for opposing Adamson in the General Election of 1924. The Reform Union, as a breakaway, had not been allowed to affiliate to the national miners' union, the Miners' Federation of Great Britain, and therefore did not receive relief funds distributed through the Federation during the 1926 struggle. During the General Strike and the miners' lock-out, Reform Union members were much more active than those of the 'Old' Union.

A big industrial struggle had almost broken out in the summer of 1925, when the miners had been threatened by the coalowners with severe reductions in their wages. But the struggle appeared to have been avoided by an eleventh-hour retreat by the Conservative government headed by Stanley Baldwin, which agreed to pay a subsidy to the coal industry to maintain miners' wages at their existing level. The subsidy was to be paid for nine months, until the end of April 1926. In the meantime, in semi-secrecy, the government began to prepare for any major industrial struggle that might come with the ending of the

Above and opposite: A mass meeting in Fife during the lock-out, addressed by A. J. Cook, General Secretary of the Miners' Federation of Great Britain.

Buckhaven Committee, Fife Miners' Reform Union, 1924. John McArthur is third from right, front row.

subsidy in the spring of 1926. It was determined never again to be caught unprepared, as it had been in 1925.

The Trades Union Congress and the unions, with some exceptions, such as the Miners' Federation, did nothing, claiming that any preparations on their part for a struggle might prejudice the chance of an agreed settlement of the crisis in the coal industry. Such a settlement, union leaders hoped, would come out of the recommendations of the Samuel Royal Commission, which had been appointed by the government soon after the crisis in 1925. To the more militant trade unionists — and of these there were strong groups among the miners of East Fife — the Samuel Commission was merely a smokescreen behind which the government was preparing for a confrontation with the miners and other unions.

At the end of April, all attempts at agreement between the miners and the coalowners having broken down, the miners were locked out until they agreed to accept severe reductions in their wages, amounting in the case of Fife and other Scots coalfields, to about 22 per cent.

Peter Fitzpatrick:

"Well, at the beginnin' o' the lock-out we got the option, whether tae work on a reduction o' wages or be locked out—that was the only alternative—fight fur our wages. So that was us locked out; and from then on it got worse."

A few days later, on 4th May, contrary to the expectations and even the wishes of the leaders of the T.U.C., the General Strike began. It was intended to demonstrate the moral and practical support by the unions as a whole for the miners in defending their wages and conditions against the coalowners' attack.

John McArthur:

"The General Strike was an event of staggering importance to all of us who had been active in the workers' movement. We had dreamt of the day when all workers would stand solid one with the other. I can remember in trying to work out what 1926 would mean—that we felt we would have to have a series of meetings in order to get our message across. I don't think many people because of bitter disappointments in the past actually felt that the General Strike would take place. The main area for holding meetings of an area character was Denbeath Bridge, and a number of us decided to hold a meeting on the Sunday prior to the General Strike. We had to cancel it for lack of attendance. But the General Strike when it took place we had a meeting the next Sunday and one could hardly see the back of the crowd."

Coal and railways were leading industries in East Fife and both were well unionised. It was therefore not surprising that, as in other industrial areas of Britain, the response to the call for a General Strike was very solid in East Fife, and that the railwaymen, road transport workers, Methil dockers, and other groups came out on strike. (Some miners also refer to their struggle in 1926 as a strike but really it was a lock-out.)

Though the miners, whose union was the largest and most militant in Britain, could draw on the relatively recent experience of their national three months' lock-out in 1921, as well as much similar experience of industrial struggle, the local organisation of the locked-out men and of the General Strikers had to be set up swiftly. This spontaneous and generally effective formation of lock-out or Strike committees, and their handling of the manifold questions that arose out of the crisis, demonstrated the resourcefulness and organising power of ordinary working people.

John McArthur:

"The period of the General Strike was a very enlightening and, looking back on it, very educative period. As the Strike developed and all loose edges were being tucked in, the Strike consolidated and a feeling of elation, of strength, of new-found strength, this solidarity of the workers, created an extraordinary atmosphere among working men, their wives and families.

"In our own area we had probably as good working-class organisation as any that had been set up. We had worked this out prior to the General Strike so that when the General Strike took place an immediate meeting of the Trades Council was called and the plan for action was laid down. The

Methil Co-operative Hall, with its ante-rooms, was taken as the Strike headquarters. It was got from the Co-op and was continuously in use, even during the night. . . .

"The Council of Action or General Strike Committee was formed by means of having a central strike committee under a convener, and each convener had a department to look after. There was a subcommittee that was in charge of permits, in charge of transport. . . . There was also the question of defence and organisation of pickets. There was built up a communications group and the East Fife Motor Club approached us and offered their services as couriers and despatch riders. This augmented the push bikes and one or two cars that were made available to us. There was the committee set up to deal with entertainment, so that there would be adequate means of keeping people entertained, preventing any question of boredom, and so on. And here we tried to get built up concert parties and groups that would do concerts and entertainment in halls or even when the weather was suitable outside entertainment as well."

William Wilson:

"I can remember the concerts very vividly—in

Kidd's Jazz Band, Leven, 1926. William 'Mosie' Murray at the piano.

fact our own Jimmy Shand, who was born and brought up just a mile down the road from Coaltown of Wemyss and here at East Wemyss, playing to concerts and also to dances."

Peter Fitzpatrick:

"Aye, aye, they'd have dances, concerts. Up at Buckhaven we used tae hae them. There's a boy cried Patrick Burns, he played the fiddle. And Brannan—he played the dulcimer. Tam Brand, he played a fiddle. And the same boys used tae gang aboot through the week, travellin' tae Dundee and Edinburgh and different places, playin' on the streets, collect money fur the soup kitchens."

As the funds of both Fife miners' unions were low, collecting money to keep the struggle going became an essential part of activity in East Fife as elsewhere.

George Simpson:

"I was in Buckhaven Town Silver Band. And we went up tae Arbroath, then on tae Dundee and then stayed in Dundee for the rest o' the week, doing the streets there. And we gathered oor collections which was totalled up every day for tae come back to East Wemyss. We went frae there, a' the villages right up the coast. At Dundee I think we finished up with £175 for the week in collections. We was in Stonehaven in the Square there for two hours playin', and we followed that wi' goin' up in Aberdeen and sleepin' in the Labour Halls off Union Street and we lay on the floor there and there were old ladies comin' in to see that we wis gettin' fed and some o' them were bringing a pitcher o' soup and we got free lunches in the Arcade and Union Street. The band broke up intae pieces, three pieces, and they went into the halls for the dancin'. We got money that way."

The best—most economical and fairest—way for the Strikers and locked-out men to organise their food supplies was by setting up communal kitchens or soup kitchens.

William Wilson:

"The village got together and we had what was known as the soup kitchen in these days and luckily for me, I was able to have two soups. I got a soup at the school and came home and my soup had been collected for me by my mother. So in fact I didn't do so badly, did I?"

The menu and amount of food available from the soup kitchens varied from one village to another, depending on the ingenuity of the organisers, the generosity of donors, or the flat refusals by some local farmers, the success of poachers, and other factors.

Alex Warrender:

"The folk was gettin' less tae eat. You were

relying on the Co-operative Society at that time to dae what I thought was a great thing—they allowed you to take credit on condition that you signed your name, that you'd pay back this amount o' credit that you had got. After the strike it was duly paid back."

Ebenezer Campbell:

"Oh, well, the soup kitchens was a godsend. Well, you was lucky if you got a plate o' soup and maybe a mashed potato or a bit o' corned beef or something like that. That's a' that could be afforded. It was a' on a sheet, ye ken, you couldna come the day and say there were fower in the family and come back in the morn and say there was just yoursel'. There was nae cheatin'."

William 'Mosie' Murray:

"Ma specific job at that particular time was to organise the soup kitchens and also provide finance. This was done successfully for a period of over seven months. And I would like to state on behalf of the traders in Leven, they were pretty good, and also the outlying farmers who supplied us with potatoes, turnips, and various other ingredients that was necessary for to make soup. The people at lunchtime came with their pitchers or their jugs and received a jugful of soup and as much bread as would do them until the following day at lunchtime. At tea time we also tried to give them a mug of tea and margarine to put on the bread which they already had. That was the staple diet of the people at that particular time. The farmers were good, but at times we couldn't receive the stuff from the farmers, so, being desperate of course, we used to go to the outlying farms and take it. That perhaps wasn't etiquette but necessity as far as I'm concerned knows no law. The main proposition was that the people had to be fed and we were determined that they would be fed."

Alex Warrender:

"Well, we were a bit luckier living near the beach because we were able to gather whelks, limpets, and mussels and bile them in cans on the beach and that gi'ed us something tae eat. For people livin' further inland couldna get that."

James Sinclair:

"They used tae get into the tattie pits and help theirsels through the night—firewood, anything that was possible to get. In fact I remember getting stopped one night wi' the policeman, carrying a five-foot pit prop down, and as you know, in the pit when ye was boring holes you used these pit props as a lance, and the policeman [says] 'Whaur are you goin' wi' that?' he says. [I] says, 'Surely get to take oor own pit prop home, that's oor born right, that's oor born right!' (laughs) I think the police were pretty sympathetic, they turned a blind

Leven miners soup kitchen staff. William 'Mosie' Murray is third left, front row.

eye to a lot. But we used to go at night and poach rabbits."

Peter Fitzpatrick:
"I've seen me comin' in wi' maybe aboot eight or ten rabbits—gie some o' them away because I knew I'd be goin' out the next day fur mair. I used tae go and do a bit o' fishin' tae. And when I came in wi' the fish I used tae gic them away. People a' helped one anither, it was the only way tae survive. Some of the farmers you couldna make them understand that you werena' on strike at a', that ye were locked out, they couldna understand that. They thought that ye were out for more money and we werena, we were just out fur tae keep what we had. But they werena wantin' you mixed up along wi' their workers in case it would cause trouble among them. I never met ony farmer yet that wis what you could say co-operative. In fact, I was along by Largo and thae places and ony farmer ye went to fur tae get stuff, they wouldna gie ye it."

Footwear became another problem, as boots and shoes wore out and it was difficult to afford repairs.

Peter Fitzpatrick:
"As far as the boots was concerned, I used tae go along the beach tae the rubbish bings. I'd gather old boots, dismantle them and take off them what would be serviceable fur us and I used tae repair other people's boots—girls from the school, boys from the school, men fur walkin' about. Some o' the men had maybe had a bit copper or two aboot them yist tae club thegither and gie me maybe threepence a piece or sixpence a piece or anything like that tae comin' on two or three bob. I used tae go along tae Kirkcaldy and buy a piece o' leather in a shop there and that was good leather fur maybe repairin' their good boots—kept us goin' in feetwear that way."

The lack of money meant lack of very basic amenities, including necessities such as razor blades.

James Sinclair:
"Black Jock was an old miner—thick black

East Wemyss miners' gala, 1926.

beard—this is how he got Black Jock. And he used to sit on his easy chair on his hunkers—you know how miners do, sit at a corner. The insurance man come in one day and Mrs Cunningham, she was away looking for the insurance book, and the insurance man, he's eyeing Jock up who hadna had a shave for a week. When Mrs Cunningham came back he says, 'Excuse me, Mrs Cunningham, but does your monkey bite?' When we told that story Jock used to go raving mad you know!" (laughs)

On 12th May, nine days after it had begun, the General Strike was suddenly and unexpectedly called off by the General Council of the T.U.C. Strikers at local level, such as East Fife, thought they were winning the struggle; they certainly did not think they were losing it. But the T.U.C. leaders, forced against their wishes to call the Strike in the first place, included a few, such as J. H. Thomas, the Railwaymen's leader, who wanted to end it as soon as possible. So great was their haste to do so that they did not even trouble to ensure that the men called out on strike in support of the miners returned to work on the same terms as before. Consequently, there were widespread attempts by employers to worsen working conditions and victimise activists—attempts which were in the main unsuccessful because even more workers came out on strike in protest, and also because the Prime Minister, Baldwin, used his influence with employers to persuade them to mitigate their attacks. The Miners' Federation refused to endorse the T.U.C.'s decision to call off the Strike, and in East Fife, as in all the other coalfields of Britain, the miners remained locked out. Though rank-and-file activists in other unions did all they could to continue practical and moral support for the miners, there was a widespread feeling that, as in 1921, the miners had been betrayed by the leaders of the other unions. For six months, from mid-May until almost the end of November, the miners struggled on courageously—but alone. Conditions became increasingly difficult. Rents went unpaid, meagre savings ran out, clothes were wearing out. In most mining villages in East Fife, the soup kitchens continued to cope efficiently; but in a few, such as Coaltown of Balgonie, where organisation was less effective or rations more meagre or there was greater isolation, the outlook became very bleak. Here and there a few miners, unable any longer to endure the privations suffered by their families, began from October onward to drift back to work. Religious belief actuated others to do so—belief which did not recognise any need for industrial struggle or even for trade unionism. But despite all difficulties the great majority of the miners in East Fife held out until their union, at national level, eventually called off the struggle toward the end of November.

Alex Warrender:
"Well, as the Strike wore on and there were no sign o' the miners gonna get the benefit of it, some people wanted to go back to work. A few of them

A Fife miner of the period.

belonging to this district got up in the mornin' and awa' to the pit. Efter a day or twa it was noticed that some folk was goin' oot ower early, so they decided to put pickets on. And I believe some of them got a bit o' a doin' afore the police was brought in to escort the blacklegs to their work. But, as far as I can mind, a lot of them was blacklisted for years after it. They maybe had a job but they never had nae freends during that time."

Harassment of the blacklegs varied in intensity from violence to humorous ridicule.

James Sinclair:
"He [the blackleg] had this pony, and the men went up one mornin', painted it aa white like a zebra, the straw hat, its ears through, slippers on its feet and tied it to the bottom o' his stair. And Ned came down in the mornin' and here's the pony

tethered to the stair and he looks at it. (laughs) John Macdonald, he made up a poem about it: 'Old Ned looks at the pony'. I can always remember the last lines, it was, 'Aince I thocht ye a gallant wee steed, But noo ye're neither a horse nor a cuddy'.

"[Another blackleg]—we called him Geordie John Jesus for a by-name, you know. We were up at Buckhaven, two or three of us one night, when Mr Bence, who kept goats—one had broken loose and it was followin' us doon the road in the dark. So we got the idea o' takin' it down and tying it on Geordie's door. And went away across the other side o' the street and lay down. When George opened the door—he's pullin' one way and the goat the other and we were lying screamin' wir heads off, watchin' the carry on! (laughs) Oh the tricks we used to play!"

George Simpson:

"I mind one old man and he had a son. His son had went oot and into the pit, and then the next mornin' he couldna get up. Somebody asked where he wis, ye ken, he kent he wisna at his work and here he was lying in his bed and his faither had hit him wi' his pit belt, ye ken, and had opened his head and he wasna able tae get up."

Peter Fitzpatrick:

"There were a terrible lot [of blacklegs]. They were comin' from Methil and they were comin' over by the beach and into the colliery. That's how they come in, direct up and through the office. And there were some o' them getting food taken down to them and kept there. They come up fur me, well, they sent a message up fur me frae the house to see if I'd come up and cut some coal fur them. I said, 'I wouldna cut a bit o' bread fur ye, never mind coal for youse.' So even after the Strike was finished, wi' me refusin' tae oblige them, they kept me idle for aboot another six or seven months for reprisals. But blacklegs, oh, you couldna count how many blacklegs they were."

Mrs Agnes Henderson:

"The next door neebour was a blackleg at Muiredge Pit, and of course he got polis protection and ah wish ye'd seen the crowds that came ahent him at that time, bringing him hame. I wouldna hae the name o' it for love nor money. It's true. Ah wouldna hae the name o' it. I'll tell ye everybody was down on him. I mind one day I was pitting out ma washing, ma bairns' nappies, and I was that roozed at him being a blackleg I went doon and I flung a stane at him one day. I was that roozed— you can imagine—well, you had nothing and he was getting a pay! And I had my claes oot and ye ken what he did? He came and he cut ma rope doon and landed all ma claes on the ground. I took ma stretcher and I battered it ower his head, so I'm tellin' you he didna half catch it for that. You can imagine thae days you had to stand up for yoursel' or if you didna you was doon the chute, you wis, you was doon the chute. Well, he maybe was a blackleg but he had to pay for it later on, for if he went oot he was like as if he was hunted; and passin' the Bank Corner a' the young men just sneered at him for a long time. But it faded away as a' thing fades away."

'Pit Bing Girls'. Miners' gala in the 1920s.

During the nine days of the General Strike and the six months of the miners' lock-out, there was sometimes conflict between the miners and the police, especially over picketing.

William 'Mosie' Murray:
"We had trouble, on one occasion we had mass pickets at the Leven station for to try and stop an incoming train that was passing through but we were met by a big contingent o' police under the auspices o' their Inspector. They immediately drew their batons and set about the pickets without getting any provocation at all."

Alex Warrender:
"Well, a beer lorry came frae, I think it was Younger's o' Alloa, making for St Andrews or some o' thae places. But it come this road. And when it got the length o' Muiredge, it turned to come doon the Wellesley road. It was stopped and was telled to turn back and he refused. So they couped the lorry. Of course barrels o' beer was burst open, and it was runnin' on the pavements and somebody went for the police and there were about twenty or thirty police come up in nae time. Several people was arrested and wheeched awa' in a van, and the rest when they saw the policeman comin, maybe me included, we run oot the road. Well, twa or three different place it happened, no' just this area."

The conflict with the police at Muiredge led the Strike committee to create a Workers' Defence Corps to protect pickets. This Corps eventually numbered 750 men, under the command of former wartime sergeant-majors and N.C.O's. It was the biggest force of its kind to be formed anywhere in Britain during the General Strike.

James Sinclair:
"They upset a beer lorry at Muiredge and the crowds were a' there, a' the men and spectators watching us. I can see the beer runnin' down the drain yet! Anyway, Inspector Clark he drew up his constables all on the one side, in front of the Co-operative, but across the road there was about four or five hundred tons of road metal and he chased the men on to the top o' this and ordered them to disperse. However, when he charged, he made the biggest mistake ever he made in his life. You could hardly see daylight for chunks o' road metal! Must have been unfortunate for him: he got hit right in the face wi' a bit. He wasna very well organised, that charge. I don't suppose there were a police

Protest march by East Fife miners to Thornton poorhouse, June 1926.

108

SOUVENIR OF THE GREAT STRIKE 1926

"ON PATROL"

Fraternally Yours, John Bird

John Bird, Bowhill (West Fife) militant miners' leader, dressed for a stunt as a 'Special Constable' in 1926.

inspector round about that was hated as much as what he was, you know."

As in every other mining area, there were a considerable number of arrests during the lock-out.

William 'Mosie' Murray:

"I was addressing a meeting at the Shorehead at Leven when I was ruthlessly hauled off the box, taken up to the local court and given thirty days' imprisonment in Saughton Jail for sedition. In the hall I was in in Saughton Jail, 'B' Hall, the whole of the Bowhill Strike Committee was incarcerated. There was John Bird and the Chairman, the Secretary, and the whole o' the committee of the Bowhill miners' union. And I may tell you, they put us through the mill. They had us out in the fields, pulling sugar beet and we never got our back up. Our food was deplorable. I'll give you the menu: in the morning they gave us a stone jar full of porridge, or lumps of porridge, no milk, that was your breakfast; at dinner time we had some watery soup, and at tea time one slice of bread an' margarine and tea without sugar or milk. That was our diet on which we had to pull sugar beet. Every week they had a concert for the inmates o' Saughton Jail but we were not allowed to attend. We were not allowed any library books or any comforts of any description. They were making sure that once you were in there you would never come back."

John McArthur:

"A foreigner—I think he was Austrian—named Kitchen, had made a foolish speech during the Strike. He was impulsive, was carried away, his English was not too good and he was arrested. The lads who were in control of the defence organisation were concerned about what was going

John McArthur, c. 1926.

Miners at work underground, Wellesley Colliery, Methil, 1926.

to happen to him, because he was not a recognised leader of the strike or the trade union movement. Although he was married locally and had a family he was not naturalised, and the question was to avoid deportation. Those lads in charge in Kirkcaldy arranged with the fiscal that he should get a nominal fine and there should be no deportation but they went back on this. He was fined and ordered to be deported. This was one of the tragedies in this area, in Kirkcaldy area especially, because this lad was deported, wandered around Europe, and finally committed suicide."

Almost seven months after it had begun, the lock-out ended in the later part of November with the defeat of the miners. No other group of workers suffered as severely as they. Their wages were reduced and their working hours lengthened from seven to eight per day. Along with the General Strike the lock-out had been the biggest labour struggle in Britain between the wars. After the calling off of the General Strike moderate trade union leaders began to declare their belief that the whole concept of a General Strike had proven a failure, though in fact it had been in many ways a remarkable demonstration of working-class support for the miners. The year 1926 proved to be a watershed for the trade unions and the broad working-class movement. From that time onward there was a

movement away from confrontation and toward greater co-operation, even collaboration, with employers and government—a movement that on the whole lasted until recent times. In the coal industry, the year 1926 left much bitterness among the miners. It made them more than ever determined to seek the nationalisation of their industry—a step taken eventually by the post-war Labour government in

Wellesley Collier, 1926.

1947. But a more immediate result of the prolonged lock-out in '26 was the victimisation by the coalowners of many of the more militant miners.

William 'Mosie' Murray:

"Now as far as myself was concerned, after the General Strike I was unable to get work of any description, any description at all. I went round the pits. I was victimised. I went to the various builders and the various other employers in Leven, but whenever my name was known as Murray, that was me out. And I was actually on the Labour Exchange for approximately six to seven year. Fortunately after that I was employed by Leven Town Council for thirty-two years."

Some of the more militant miners who were victimised were forced to find work as best they could. Some became local insurance agents; others as 'shilling-a-week men', or door-to-door salesmen. Quite a few of those victimised were forced to leave the East Fife coalfield altogether in search of work. Some of them emigrated to Canada, Australia or the United States; others moved to pits in other coalfields in Scotland or England. Most of those who were victimised but remained in East Fife remained active in the miners' union and in one or other of the three main political parties that enjoyed the support of the miners:

the Labour Party, Communist Party or Independent Labour Party. Some in due course became burgh or Fife county councillors, leading figures in the local Co-operative Societies, respected the more for the suffering they had undergone and the leadership they had given in '26. But whether they remained or moved away, East Fife miners, like tens of thousands elsewhere who had struggled through the lock-out, looked back on 1926 as the most memorable year of their lives. A good deal of the reputation for industrial militancy which today still attaches to miners was earned for them by their long drawn out struggle in 1926. Often closely knit communities living at some distance from more urbanised workers, miners had over many decades of hard working and living conditions developed strong loyalties and powers of endurance that made it difficult for some other people to understand what they saw as mere stubbornness and almost mindless militancy.

Peter Fitzpatrick:

"Ah think they were a pretty reasonable, honest set o' people, the miners. In fact, I've never met a class o' people as reasonable and understandin' as what the minin' class wis. People away frae the pits that never wis near them thinks that the miners had horns on their head but it's no true."

IAN MacDOUGALL

David Proudfoot, a leading militant miner, speaking in front of banner during the 1926 struggle.

Glasgow Jewry

Jews have lived in Glasgow at least from the beginning of the nineteenth century. It is thought that the earliest Jewish inhabitant was Isaac Cohen who purchased his Burgess Certificate to trade as a hatter in 1812. He was joined by Jews who were engaged in a wide variety of occupations in the city: merchants, agents and auctioneers, optical and mathematical instrument makers, furriers, jewellers, manufacturers of 'French Fancy Goods' and makers of artificial flowers. James Cleland, writing in 1831, made the following observations on the newly established community:

"A Jews' Synagogue was opened in this city in September 1823, Mr Moses Lisenheim is their Priest, Hebrew Teacher and Killer [*shochet*—a Jewish butcher authorised to kill animals according to the Laws of Shechita]. The Feast of Tabernacles, which used to be celebrated by the Glasgow Jews in Edinburgh, is now observed in this City. A Burial Ground is about to be opened in Hutchesontown for the interment of the Seed of Abraham. Edward Davies, son of Mr Edward Davies, Optician, was the first that was circumcised in Glasgow; the rite was performed by Mr Michael on 18th July 1824. . . . The Jews are 47 in number, viz. Males, 28 — Females, 19; above 20 years of age, 28 — below do., 19. Born in the following countries, viz.:— in Prussian Poland, 11 — in various parts of Germany, 12 — in Holland, 3 — in London, 5 — in Sheerness, 10 — and in Glasgow, 6."

Growth was slow and in 1860 it was estimated that there were still only twenty-six Jewish families resident in Glasgow. The community, though small, was conspicuous by its success and according to one contemporary, non-Jewish writer, displayed all the virtues of mid-Victorian respectability: "The Jews in Glasgow . . . are moral, industrious, educated and some of them wealthy. . . ." The majority of the Jews lived north of the Clyde and it was not until the mid-1870s and 1880s, with the arrival of immigrants from Eastern Europe, that expansion into the south side of the city, and into the Gorbals area in particular, took place. By the end of the 1880s the centre of the Jewish population had shifted away from the Garnethill area, where a substantial new synagogue had been built in 1879, towards the densely populated Gorbals district where accommodation was cheaper and life undoubtedly rougher. It was more than the waters of the Clyde that separated the wealthy, well-educated, anglicized Jews of Garnethill from the 'greeners' of the south side.

Opposite: A Jewish cap-making factory, Oxford Street, Gorbals, c. 1915.

Most of the newcomers were Yiddish-speaking Jews of Russian and Polish extraction seeking refuge from the religious and economic persecution that was the lot of the Jews under Tsarist rule.

Mrs Braverman:
"I come frae Dubna *guberniya* in Russia and I was born, I think, in 1891. I remember I was always running around, going to the market. It was in a big square and the old ladies used to sit with their shawls round them, freezing cold, and they'd sit by a fired top and warm their hands. The potatoes used to be roast on there and some people would bring a pot and take maybe six potatoes home. . . . Everybody was poor. The pogroms were gettin' so bad that I was told they used to go into a house and they'd pull a baby's tongue out! I was told that and I felt terrible and I thought I'd like to go down to the barracks to see what these people looked like but they were just ordinary soldiers. Anyway, people were nervous in case things got worse and that's the reason they left because things weren't so good."

Mr Stone:
"My folks were married in Suwalki, that's in Lithuania. They were penniless. Round about 1880 it was enacted that all Jews were liable for military service. Well, there was the difficulty with the dietary laws bein' infringed and they wanted time for worshippin', so they decided to get out. The problem was how to get over the border. My mother related that the young girls would chat to the border guards while the rest of the Jews skipped over. Once you had a foot over the border that was you safe, you were in Prussia. They hitchhiked tae Hamburg and the main thing tae notice, they'd practically no food. Water, herring, and black bread, that sustained them. It was pure chance whether the ship arrived in Leith, Cardiff or Liverpool."

Some may have used Glasgow merely as a staging point for their ultimate destination, America, *die goldene medine*, the golden land. Others had settled elsewhere in Britain and had come to the Gorbals via London, Manchester, Leeds, Newcastle and also Dundee and Edinburgh. It was estimated that in 1903, of a total Jewish population of 6,000, about 4,000 lived in the Gorbals district alone. Visible evidence of their presence was not difficult to find. There were synagogues in Oxford Street and South Portland Street, the latter built at a cost of £9,000, a *Talmud Torah* school (a religious education school) with a roll of about 400 in Buchan Street. In Oxford Street there was

Three Jewish upholsterers, the Gorbals, c. 1915.

a 'Zionist Free Reading Room and Library' and in Portugal Street, the Glasgow Hebrew Benevolent Loan Society had premises which opened shortly after its foundation in 1888. In addition, there were more than sixty Jewish stores and workshops in the vicinity.

Mrs Aitken:
"It was nearly all Jewish shops and Jewish firms in the Gorbals. There was the Fogels, the corner of Hospital Street and Cleland Street, there was the Jewish bakery at the corner of Dunmore Street. Gleicken, the gown people were there and the Ashers as well. The Gerbers, the Woolfsons, them that had all the jewellers, the shops in the Trongate, they came from there. There were small cabinet-making businesses and upholstery work right up to Cumberland Street. . . . Some o' them kept stock in one o' their rooms for customers to come up and see what they wanted and they could get them everything. They all opened little shops, just doing alterations and repairs to suits and everything. There was no provident checks or anything like that, everybody had a wee connection of giving credit and goin' to collect it. It was a great place the Gorbals."

Mr Grossman:
"Gorbals Cross on a Sunday mornin'. That was a wonderful thing! If you wanted to meet anybody you just went along to Gorbals Cross. Well, there were different groups—tailors, cabinet-makers, travellers, and so on—and they'd all be discussing different things, their trades, politics, football. There would be crowds all over, every Sunday mornin'."

A considerable proportion of the occupied male population were self-employed and many of the small-scale businesses that were set up in this period were financed through loans supplied by the Glasgow Hebrew Benevolent Loan Society. In 1901, for example, the Society granted 175 loans.

Mr Glasser:
"These loans were granted free of interest mainly to pedlars and travellers and that gave them the basis for making a living from the stock that they could buy and sell. They used to go to the outside of Glasgow, to Uddingston, Baillieston and into the mining communities like Hamilton, Coatbridge and Airdrie to sell their wares. They were selling various things, braces, mouth-organs, games, small things that needed small money for stock. When they became a little wealthier they paid the money back. Two people out of the community, who were more affluent, would sign as guarantors so that the fund would never be depleted by loss."

On occasion, capital could also be obtained from some of the wealthier and more established members of the community. Initially, profit margins were low.

Mr Tobias:
"They had a hard, hard life at the beginning. Ma father told us that he used to get up at maybe three or four o'clock in the morning and rush down to the Gorbals to see if he'd missed the time to go to his work. They'd no clock, nothing! The poverty was absolutely diabolical. He had a trade, he was a blacksmith and he worked for twelve years for this company and the boss was a real slave-driver! . . . Well, he went to a firm in Glasgow, a Jewish company of merchants called Shaunfield & Co., Hope Street and they supplied him with an anvil and bellows and equipment to start up on his own. They supplied him with steel to do the work and some of the merchants gave him a little credit. He

Mr Tobias and some of the work force.

A Jewish bakery in Main Street, Gorbals, c. 1910.

started his own business in 1900 in MacFarlane Street in the Gallowgate and many a week he'd come home with hardly a penny in his pocket after he'd paid one or two bills. It wasn't easy going."

Mrs Taylor:
"My husband was a traveller in the credit drapery line. He owed half o' Glasgow I think (laughs). Later he started to go out and canvas for gold, old gold bullion and he did quite well. Then he was selling watches, clocks, jewellery, he'd buy up stock in shops that were giving up and he'd clean and polish it up and take it to the 'Barras' to sell. Oh, if I had £2 in a week I was lucky. We always kept a few pounds back for his stock but I was always diggin' into it! Yes, you could get help from the Board of Guardians or the Parish but we would never think of going to these places. No. We just took what we could get and just struggled away."

There were some among the immigrant community, however, who required this kind of basic assistance. In 1901, for instance, the two main relief organisations in Glasgow, the Jewish Board of Guardians and the Hebrew Ladies' Benevolent Society, between them dealt with over 500 needy cases. It was a measure of the degree of poverty that existed among the foreign Jews that a number of additional relief organisations were set up in the 1890s and early 1900s. These included the Boot and Clothing Guild, the Sick Visiting Association, the *Hachnosas Orchin* (society for welcoming strangers) and the *Hachnosas Kalla* (society for providing the bride with a dowry). Collectively, the objective was the same, namely, 'to promote self-respect and independence among the recipients of help'.

These organisations were remarkably successful in that few immigrant Jews found their way onto the parish relief books. The allegation, frequently made during the chauvinistic campaign which led to the Aliens Act of 1905, that the Jewish immigrants were adding to the local rates burden was thus refuted in Glasgow. Nonetheless, the sudden appearance of, what was thought to be, a large Jewish immigrant population, quite different in status and background from their respected co-religionists, created unease. There was opposition to the group as Jews and as immigrants.

As early as 1893, J. A. Hammerton in his *Sketches from Glasgow* was depicting the quintessential Jewish stereotype:

"He has a rather sallow complexion, and his face is fringed with straggling black whiskers. He wears a frock coat that was black in the long ago. He is earnestly conversing with a fair companion, rather gaudily attired, but good looking for her nationality. ... A glance at him is sufficient to proclaim him a son of Israel. He is a money-lender in the city — like not a few of his tribe — and his conversation has reference, no doubt, to some advantageous bond he has received."

As the *Jewish Chronicle* was later to remark: 'Take away the stilted style and the writing of this passage hardly shows a very agreeable spirit.' One area where this manifested itself was in house-letting.

Mr Stone:
"Before the First World War it was very, very hard for a Jew to get a house. One landlord after another: 'No Jews!'. If your name was Finkleberg then he'd say, 'No'. So you just changed it to Faulkner or something and if you didn't have a semitic nose then you might get it."

Occasionally, the Jews came under attack because of their religion. In a period when the Churches were heavily involved in 'mission-work' at home and abroad it did not pass unnoticed that an 'Eastern quarter' had appeared in the midst of the city. To counter any 'threat' a Glasgow Jewish Evangelical Mission was established in 1907 and there were also visits paid to the city by members of the Society for the Propagation of the Gospel to the Jews. One of the major criticisms concerned the Jewish violation of the Sabbath, a theme also taken up by the trade unions in the campaign to prohibit Sunday trading.

Sabbatarianism provided a useful front for what was essentially an economic grievance — excessively long working hours. In a submission to the Trades Council in June 1908 the Glasgow and District Furniture Trades' Federation concluded:

". . . we think we ought to have secure protection that our valued Sunday shall not be broken down and trampled underfoot by the unthinking foreigner in his greedy pursuit of financial gain."

It was the exploitation of cheap immigrant labour and the threat which this posed to working hours ('our valued Sunday') and to wages that was the main concern of the unions. The need for protection was not lost to the immigrants themselves. For example, in 1905 an Independent Jewish Cabinetmakers' Association was set up only to collapse the following year when its meagre funds were exhausted after a three-weeks long dispute with a group of Jewish employers over Sunday working. More successful was the International Tailors', Machinists' and Pressers' Union established in 1894 in Crown Street, Gorbals, and with a membership of over 220 by 1902. In a dispute in the same year the union succeeded in winning a 15 per cent increase in piece-rates and in the following year supported the Tailors' Society in their nine-month long strike. This type of behaviour made an important contribution to the gradual process of integration.

Most of the Jews who were involved in trade unions were also active politically. Zionism, which was still only in its infancy in the early 1900s, attracted a great deal of support in Glasgow and, indeed, in later years it was said that Zionism had 'all the force of a religious creed' among the Glasgow community. It was through the Workers' Circle (Arbeiter Ring) that much of the political activity was channelled.

Mr Glasser:
"There was a branch in Main Street, Gorbals [c. 1915]. Downstairs there was the communal baths and the 'steamy', where you washed your clothes, and the top flat was rented by the Workers' Circle. The activities were two-fold. One was associated with Poale Zion, that's the Zionist workers and this organisation was linked to the Labour Party and a number were members of that. There were others, quite separate, who were essentially interested in

their social welfare. They would negotiate better conditions, shorter hours, time off for Shabbos [Sabbath] and so on. There were quite a number integrated into the socialist parties. There were members of the I.L.P., the Independent Labour Party, the B.S.P., the British Socialist Party, and the S.L.P., the Socialist Labour Party—these were different grades of socialism."

Mr Stone:
"The Workers' Circle, aye, they were very active workers. They turned out some worthy people, men like Manny Shinwell, you know. He, along with what they later called the 'Red Clydesiders'—Kirkwood, Geordie Buchanan, Jimmy Maxton—these fellas had no hesitation in comin' and givin' us a wee talk. Jimmy Maxton, I remember him tellin' us that when he went to school he saw the utter futility of teaching a class o' children that had no boots and were obviously without any breakfast. Och, the sufferings of the poor Jews wasn't any more than the sufferings of the Glasgow underfed population."

It was possibly because they shared in the poverty that surrounded them that there was, by all accounts, little active opposition to the Jews at street or tenement close level. Communal relations appear to have been little different to those experienced by other 'foreigners', whether from Ireland, Italy, Lithuania or Edinburgh. The immigrant Jews in fact lived a fairly self-contained and independent existence, well organised but poor, tolerated but not accepted.

In the early days some of the customs imported from the shtettl in Eastern Europe were maintained in a community characterised by its orthodoxy.

Mr Grossman:
"There were marriage-brokers, shadchans, they brought boy and girl together. It was more common then than it is now, you never hear of it now. The weddin's all took place in the synagogues. Oh, they were lovely weddin's, class, real class. A Jewish wedding in those days was catered by the local Jewish butcher, there was an odd one that was catered outside but no' many. It would be under the supervision of a shomer, a man who looks after these things. They were really good. The best hall in those days was the Trades House in Glassford Street, that was supposed to be a nice class wedding."

Mrs Aitken:
"Our parents, they were very strict with us. There's only one in our family out of ten children that married out. In those days it was a terrible thing to do. We never got going out on a Friday night until after ma parents were gone. My father would be readin' his Talmud [the main Rabbinical text] and we would be in the room just havin' a talk with some other friends. The neighbours would come in for a little while and that'd be it. On

Oxford Star F.C., 1910. Top left: Mr Grossman.

Saturday we were so modern that we went out. We did our bit o' shoppin', and brought the messages in and quietly put them away *then* we went in and spoke to ma parents! (laughs)"

Strict observance was also displayed in other areas of community life.

Mr Grossman:

"I was president then [1910] of the 'Oxford Star' football team. You couldnae meet a nicer set o' boys, they were all Jewish boys who lived around Oxford Street in the Gorbals. I don't think we played on the Sabbath. Well, we never played near the Gorbals, if we did play we played away in another district. I may tell you the candid truth we'd hundreds o' people used to come and watch us. That was a regular occasion."

Mr Glasser:

"They went on holiday to places like Dunoon, Innellan and Rothesay, these were the places in the early part of the century. If you were orthodox and observed all the ritual dietary laws then you had to carry all the various utensils in a hamper: pots, pans, crockery and linen as well for the beds. You couldn't go down without having a *minyan*, that is, ten people to make up a prayer meeting. As most of the families weren't very affluent, the father would return to Glasgow and do his work for the week and come back on the Friday before the Sabbath. He'd bring some food, among which was the black bread, the salt herring, and the *chala* [a twisted loaf of white bread], small pieces that were suitable for the Sabbath along with the wheaten loaf. The loaf

was used for making the *Kaddish*, the prayer for bringing in the Sabbath and the prayer of the blessing of the bread. It was observed strictly and with due diligence and care just as if you were at home."

Much depended on the attitude and influence of the parents for the new generation were being exposed daily to a culture which at points challenged their *Yiddishkeit* (Jewishness). A major problem was the absence of a Jewish day school.

Mr Grossman:

"I went to Rose Street School. They were nearly all Jewish children and we used to come in half-an-hour later than the rest o' them because they said their prayers at that time. In those days we didn't say any prayers to my knowledge—I might be wrong, mind ye, maybe I was too late in gettin' into school! We had teachers to teach us the various things and we went to little *chedarim* [small, traditional, religious schools] and they maybe had some pupils. Other times you might have a teacher come to the house to teach you, you were lucky if it was a twenty-minute lesson and then he dashed away to another house. That was quite common in my day and I was born in Glasgow in 1885."

The establishment of the *Talmud Torah* school in 1895 improved the provision for instruction in Hebrew and religious education but, although the number on the roll remained consistently high, it is difficult to determine the level and regularity of attendance at classes held three times a week after school hours. Few children in the Gorbals district, Jew or Gentile, would

have relished the prospect of extra schooling.
Some Jewish children experienced other problems of
an equally 'serious' nature.

Mrs Woolfson:
"When I was at school I was challenged by one
of my friends and I was asked whether I was a
Protestant or a Catholic and I said, 'No, I'm a Jew.'
So I was then asked whether I was a Protestant Jew
or a Catholic Jew. Well, I went to a Protestant
school so I said, 'I'm a Protestant Jew!' (laughs)"

Mr Latter:
"I was playing for the Southern Y.M.C.A. at the
time and we were in the amateur cup, doing quite
well and thinking that possibly we might win it.
We'd won our previous round and then some guy
produced a protest against me. He dug up this old
rule that if you played for the Y.M.C.A. ye had to
have two consecutive attendances in the Bible
Class! Well, I was desperate because I really
thought we'd a chance o' winning this cup. I
thought about it and decided to go. Surely it canna
be all that bad, I'll no' open ma mouth, no' sing any
hymns or anything like that. So when I went I sat
at the back, kept my mouth shut the whole time,
expecting a bolt from heaven to come down and
strike me (laughing). I made my two appearances
and that meant I could carry on playin' for the
Southern Y.M.C.A. Anyway, this guy must have got
the needle and thought that he'd have tae try
something different. So he sent an anonymous letter
to my aunt and this was eventually passed on to my
Dad. In the letter it said, 'If you want to find your
son on a Saturday afternoon you'll find him in
Glasgow Green playin' for the Southern Y.M.C.A.
and if ye wonder where he gets to on a Sunday
night, he's at the Bible Class!' Ye can imagine, it
caused ructions in the family. It would be a fairy-
tale end to say that we won the cup but we were
knocked out in the next round (laughing)."

By the 1920s and 1930s aspects of the old way of life
had changed and in some cases disappeared altogether
as increasingly the younger generation adopted the
habits and culture of the host society. Yiddish, for
example, which had been spoken in most houses, was
doomed to extinction. One Yiddish newspaper after
another folded—the daily, *Evening Times*, the bi-lingual
monthly, *Jewish Life* — until finally in 1928 the weekly
Jewish Voice succumbed to become the *Jewish Echo*, the
Glasgow community's English language newspaper.
Only the middle aged and elderly took advantage of the
large collection of Yiddish and Hebrew books
(estimated at over 1,000 in 1934) in the new Gorbals
library. There was a much greater laxity in Sabbath
observance, for those in business adopted a more
pragmatic approach and many of them kept their shops
open on Saturdays. It was not unusual to find Jewish
supporters on the terraces at Ibrox, Parkhead or
Cathkin Park, home of the now defunct Third Lanark.

Mr Latter:
"There was quite a good support for the Thirds,
whether some of it was due to me being Jewish and
playin' for them I don't know. The fact that I was
playin' on a Saturday was no different to somebody
having to keep their shop open on a Saturday to
earn a living and, of course, I was gettin' good
money. Even though I was playin' on the Sabbath I
was a sort of wee tin god because I was playin'
professional football and possibly enhancing the
Jewish image as it were."

The theatre, the cinema and the dance-hall all drew
large Jewish crowds. These were venues that in
previous years would have been out of bounds and
regarded as inappropriate and potentially harmful to
the orthodox Jew. Yet, Jews not only owned some of
them but performed in them as well.

Mr Tobias:
"There were two comedians, Peel and Curtis,
they were on for a long time. They were quite
famous and were heard all over the English circuit
as well. Peel and Curtis, Blass and Spilg, these were
their original Jewish names. Then there was a
young man called Ike Freedman, his real name was
Solomons, and he came from the East End of
Glasgow and he was very popular amongst the
Glasgow people. He used to perform in the Palace
Theatre, the Metropole and went round most of the
circuits. . . . Oh, there were plenty of jokes about
the Jewish people in Glasgow but they were all
taken in good part. It was give and take on most
occasions."

Humour was, of course, one way of coping with
injustice and prejudice which the Jews encountered.
For although the immigrant community had travelled
far along the road towards acceptance there remained
a suspicion, an antipathy towards the group.

Mr Stone:
"I got the sack for being a Jew! The war was on,
this was 1916, and the boss come in and says 'I don't
want a German Jew' and told me to get out. I was
born in this country. . . . Well eventually I found
myself in the army and I remember when I got to
the barracks there was a Jewish lad on duty serving
out the breakfasts. He was dishin' it out with a big
ladle. You just had to take what you got, bacon and
all. And there was this big hefty lad sitting opposite
me and he shouted, 'You bloody Jews make sure
you get the best.' So this fella just put down his big
tray and he belted, really clobbered this chap. The
fella next to me turned round and asks, 'You know
who that is?', and I says, 'No'. He says, 'That's
Myer Stringer, the Scottish boxing champion'. . . .
Because of the provocation Myer was exonerated
and they realised they might as well make use of
him so they made him a gym instructor!"

Prejudice was not as easily handled in peace-time. The Churches, for example, still continued to display evidence of intolerance in their treatment of Jews. To cite but one example, in March 1938, at a time when the newspapers were full of accounts of the suffering of the Jewish population in Germany and Austria, the Moderator-Designate of the General Assembly of the Church of Scotland, in a speech entitled *The Enigma of the Jew*, commented:

> ". . . there are only two ways to treat the Jews, and they are to fight them or to convert them, and Britain's desire is not to fight them but to see them converted to accepting the pure and unsophisticated principles of the Christian religion as their faith."

This unwillingness to accept the Jews in their own right occurred elsewhere. There were bowling clubs, for example, in Glasgow, which refused to accept Jewish members, and it was because of discrimination that Jewish golfers founded their own club, Bonnyton Golf Club, in 1928. In housing there was the case which George Buchanan, I.L.P. M.P. for the Gorbals, brought before the House of Commons on 12th February 1935. It concerned the refusal by one of Glasgow's leading builders to allocate a house in the new King's Park estate on the grounds that the person 'belonged to the Jewish race'. The company policy was changed almost immediately but the ignorance that lay behind it was deep-rooted and was to persist.

It would be misleading to exaggerate the importance of anti-semitic feeling in the inter-war years but foolish to ignore it. It may well have contributed to the rapid growth in the number of Jewish organisations in this period, particularly Zionist groups. Its effect on the community must, however, have been tempered by the knowledge that on the continent the plight of the Jews was much worse. News of the persecution of the German Jews led in August 1933 to a boycott of German goods in the city and almost overnight a whole series of relief organisations sprang up. Support came from a number of quarters, from Willie Gallagher, the Communist Party member to Lord Marley and Mrs Anthony de Rothschild, all of whom appeared at protest and fund-raising meetings in Glasgow. From 1933 onwards refugees began to arrive.

Mr Glasser:
"We had an organisation in Glasgow known as the Central British Fund for the Relief of German Jews, there was also an organisation set up by the members of the Federation of Women Zionists, it was known as the Glasgow W.I.Z.O. The refugees who came over here were sponsored by Jewish families and became members of the family until they managed to get resettled. The children were dispersed in two's and three's throughout the community. There were quite a number of professional people among the refugees, doctors and dentists and so forth. For example, in 1934, Dr Karl Abenheimer arrived in Glasgow. He had an extensive knowledge of psychotherapy and psycho-analysis and was quite outstanding. He was so proficient that he taught the doctors here because psychoanalysis was practically unknown until he came here. . . . Bringing the children over, well, it affected every individual because you realised what was happening."

Most of the refugees were from Germany and Austria. There were some who came from further afield, for example, from Singapore, but they were sponsored in the same way.

Mrs Simon:
"When we arrived in Glasgow the billeting officer said, 'Have you got any relatives here?' I said, 'I have one person and that is God' (laughs). We were taken to the Beresford Hotel and then to the Y.W.C.A. It was our Passover and I told my daughters that they're not to eat bread. I didn't know you could get *matzos* here. So the matron phoned Mr Glasser and sent us to Geneen's Kosher Hotel in Abbotsford Place and they were wonderful to us. The whole Passover week was paid by Geneen's."

Geneen's Kosher Hotel, c. 1928, regarded as the centre of the Jewish community.

Calderwood Lodge Primary children: the Festival of Succot.

The sponsorship scheme worked efficiently and well and the newcomers who decided to settle here adapted to life in Glasgow with apparently little difficulty. The Jewish community, by this time, was quite widely dispersed for the drift away from the Gorbals had started almost as soon as family finances would permit. The movement was always to the south of the city: first to Govanhill, then to Battlefield and Shawlands and later to Newton Mearns, Netherlee, Clarkston and Giffnock. The poorest Jews remained in the Gorbals as did the Jewish shops, workshops and warehouses.

Mrs Taggart:
"I came from Palestine as they called it then in 1944 because I had married a Glasgow fella, he was a soldier. I went first to his parents' house in Parkhead and then we went to the Gorbals to Thistle Street. There were quite a few Jewish families but I couldnae speak to them—they couldnae speak Hebrew and I couldnae speak Yiddish! I was there about eleven years in that house, it was only a single-end, a sub-let really, but I really liked the Gorbals there, really friendly people. I used to get fruit really cheap. There was this man with a fruit barrow and 'cos I come from Palestine he used to give me oranges and all kinds of fruit cheap. One day he saw me walking along the street and he stopped me and told me that there's a horse running by the name of 'Palestine' and that I should back it. I did and he won, he won the Derby! . . . It was the shopping I really liked. If I wanted any Jewish food, I went to the Jewish shops, especially the Jewish bakeries, they were really beautiful. On a Sunday morning standing in a queue to buy the cakes and muffins from the Jewish shop. We used to look forward to Sunday mornings!"

With the massive redevelopment of the Gorbals in the 1960s the last vestiges of a Jewish presence in the area disappeared. In 1965, the Board of Guardians set up a special house-purchase scheme to help needy families and those who were living in substandard houses in the Gorbals area were moved elsewhere, to be replaced by Punjabi and Kashmiri immigrants from the Indian subcontinent. Today, in an area which was once a leading centre of Zionism, there is now a large mosque under construction, evidence of yet another phase of immigration.

The Glasgow Jewish community, estimated to be 11,000 to 12,000 strong, is centred now in Giffnock, a district occupied almost entirely by members of the professional and business classes. The social and economic division of a hundred years ago no longer exists, or at least not to the same extent, and in terms of associations and societies, the community has never been better organised. There remains, however, the thorny problem of assimilation.

Dr Jesner:
"There are many groups in the community and the umbrella organisation is the Glasgow Jewish Representative Council which represents all the organisations in the West of Scotland. There are welfare organisations: the Jewish Welfare Board, the Jewish Old Age Home, the Association for the Mentally Handicapped, the Blind Society. There are religious organisations, the synagogues, the Ritual Council which looks after the ritual slaughtering of the meat, and the *Beth Din* [Jewish Ecclesiastical Court]. There are many other organisations such as the Friends of the Hebrew University, the Jewish Graduates Group, the Association of Jewish Ex-Servicemen, the *Yeshiva* [a Jewish learning centre], the Zionists, the Jewish Choral Society and so on. . . . Yet I don't think the community is as religious as it was a generation ago. There has been some inter-marriage and I think there's little doubt that inter-marriage has been increasing. Most of the Jewish community are displeased by this because they feel that it is undermining the strength of the community and weakening the threads of the history of the community."

Mr Tobias:
"There's only one progressive synagogue in Glasgow that takes in the people who have mixed marriages—it's an easy outlet for them. I've never been in a progressive synagogue because I'm completely orthodox and I'd like ma family to follow me. Ma daughter is very orthodox but ma son's not so hot! He won't do any harm so long as

I'm here, I know he won't do anything to upset me. Well, he's forty-seven now and I'm now seventy-seven (laughs)."

Mr Stone:

"You've got assimilation now. I'm not sayin' anything for it or against it but that is the position. Then there's Sabbath observance, well that's no' in the same class as before. I'm sure if you went down to Bonnyton Golf Club you'd find quite a congregation there on the Sabbath. Where you will see it is during the festivals then you'll see the synagogues crowded but for the rest, no.''

An important development in the struggle to maintain the Jewish faith and Jewish culture was the establishment of the first Jewish day school in Glasgow in 1962.

Mrs Woolfson:

"I think there were about nineteen in the first class, today we've got about 220 in the school. We have eight classes plus a nursery and teach the full range of primary subjects. In addition, we have all the Jewish subjects, the Hebrew language, spoken and written. Bible study, our traditions and festivals. We actually participate in the festivals as they come through the year so the children are actually living their Judaism as well as learning it from books.''

Education of this kind undoubtedly creates a greater awareness among the children of being Jewish and it will be further enhanced by the plethora of Jewish youth groups and societies set up for that purpose. For their parents and grandparents, apart from their own religious beliefs, external events have produced the same effect. The Balfour Declaration of 1919, the tragedy of the Holocaust, which, as Dr Jesner has said, 'coloured our whole way of life', the creation of the State of Israel in 1948 have contributed to raising the level of Jewish consciousness. It has not, however, prevented the Glasgow Jews from making a major contribution to the life of the city in, for example, politics, business and medicine. Nor has it created any conflict of loyalty.

Mrs Woolfson:

"I think that Jews very much identify themselves with the place of their birth. I feel very Scottish and I'm very happy to be in Scotland and have a little foothold in Israel as well for my daughter was married there recently. Funnily enough, there's quite a large community of Scots in Israel, and it really came to the fore last year when they held a Burns Supper and the people clamoured to take part!''

Mr Glasser:

"Let me put it to you this way. There are five million Scots living in Scotland and there are about twenty million Scots living outside the country. In all these places, Canada, America, New Zealand, there are Scots societies called 'Sons of Scotia', Burns clubs and so on. St Andrew's Day is celebrated and the people identify with Scotland. They talk of the 'motherland' but they are loyal to the country that they're living in. The Jews in this country are likewise.''

The transition from being a Jew in Scotland to being a Scottish Jew may not, at times, have been easy, but it seems by now to be completed.

Mr Stone:

"I mind when I had that experience here of being turfed out o' my job for bein' a Jew. I said to myself maybe I'd be better gettin' out of this country. Well, I haven't left yet 'cos I don't know a better one (laughs). I'll tell ye something interestin' now. In that wonderful Mitchell Library we've got here in Glasgow—it's a veritable paradise—you can go in there and find not only English but Scottish poetry translated into Hebrew. I came across this Burns collection translated by a Tel Aviv fellow. And it really gave me a great thrill to see 'Auld Lang Syne' printed in Hebrew. I'm no' much of a singer but it goes like this:

עָבְרוּ יָמִים מִכְּבָר (Auld Lang Syne)

יַחְדָּו עַל פֶּלֶג שָׁטְנוּ אָז	עָבְרוּ יָמִים מִכְּבָר
כָּל עוֹד הַיּוֹם זָהַר;	הֲיִשָּׁכַח יָדִיד קָדוּם
הִרְעִימוּ רַחֲבֵי־יַמִּים —	וְלֹא יְהִי נִזְכָּר?
עָבְרוּ יָמִים מִכְּבָר.	הֲיִשָּׁכַח יָדִיד קָדוּם
הַפִּזְקֹהֵלָה:	מִן הַיָּמִים מִכְּבָר?
לְזֵכֶר הַיָּמִים עָבְרוּ... וכו'	
	הַפִּזְקֹהֵלָה:
	לְזֵכֶר הַיָּמִים עָבְרוּ,
יָדִי לְךָ; הַב לִי יָדְךָ,	לְזֵכֶר הַיָּמִים,
רֵעִי נֶאֱמָן־יָקָר!	כּוֹס־חֶסֶד עוֹד נָרִים יַחְדָּו
לְךָ, נִשָּׂא כּוֹס שֶׁל בְּרָכָה	לְזֵכֶר הַיָּמִים...
לְזֵכֶר יְמֵי־כְבָר!	
הַפִּזְקֹהֵלָה:	אַהַבְנוּ רוּץ בֵּינוֹת הָרִים,
לְזֵכֶר הַיָּמִים עָבְרוּ... וכו'	אֲרוֹת פְּרָחִים בַּכָּר,
	אַךְ רֶגֶל זֶה בָּצִקָה, צִיְפָה —
כּוֹס רְוָיָה לְךָ נָלִי,	עָבְרוּ יָמִים מִכְּבָר.
נֵיטִיב הַלֵּב, נָשָׂבְרָ!	הַפִּזְקֹהֵלָה:
כּוֹס־חֶסֶד בּוֹא נָרִים יַחְדָּו	לְזֵכֶר הַיָּמִים עָבְרוּ... וכו'
לְזֵכֶר יְמֵי־כְבָר!	

רוֹבֶּרְט בָּרְנְס [ROBERT BURNS]

MURDOCH RODGERS

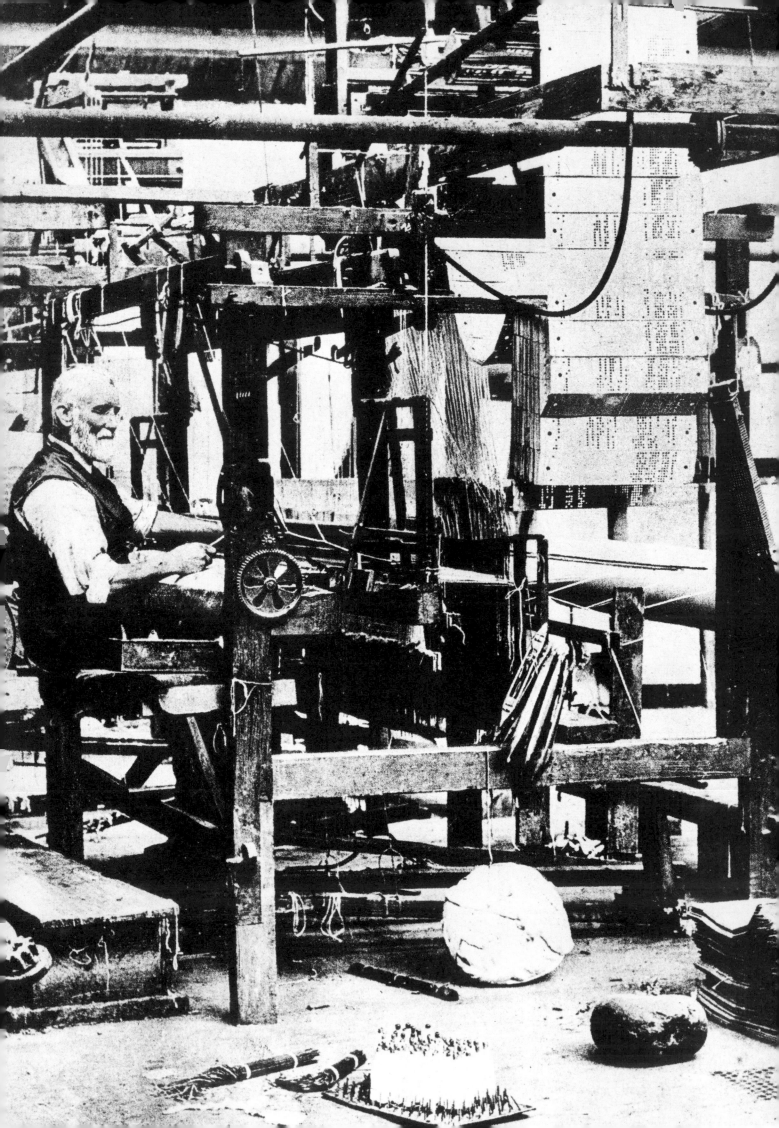

Up the Valley

The men and women who work in the lace factories of Ayrshire's Irvine Valley are heir to a long tradition of skilled weaving. The Galston Kirk records of the 1570s mention both walkers and wabsters living in the parish, weaving wool spun locally and brought to them by the customer. Local tradition has it that Protestant Flemish and French Huguenot refugees settled in the Valley in the later sixteenth and early seventeenth centuries, introducing the advanced draw loom and the skills of pattern weaving. Typical Valley surnames such as Scade, Frame, Gebbie, Howie and Fleming probably arrived with these immigrant groups, and 400 years later the same names will be found among the lace, madras, terylene and silk weavers of Newmilns and Darvel.

Woollen goods continued to be woven in Galston well into this century, but for the Valley as a whole, wool was eclipsed by linen manufacture arising from Government aid after 1727. The wealth generated by the linen industry was such that Newmilns built a fine Town House in 1739, and farmers' sons were attracted into the older burghs in such numbers that the 'new town' of Darvel was established in 1751 to house the increase in population. The linen boom was also aided by the improvement in roads following the Turnpike Act of 1766, which facilitated the supply of outside flax

to the Valley lint mills, and the transport of the finished article to the merchants of Glasgow and Paisley. Increased contact with these larger manufacturing districts also led to the introduction and eventual specialisation in finer fancy goods. The first silk loom was set up in Galston in 1781. By 1791 forty out of fifty-five of the town's looms were engaged in producing this luxury article. The availability of cheap cotton from India and the improvement in the thread spun on Crompton's mule led also to a specialisation in fine muslin weaving in the 1790s. Many Ayrshire women augmented the family income by engaging in tambour work, sewing beautifully intricate lace insertions into the muslin gauze woven by the man of the house and eventually fashioned into the flowing gossamer gowns which adorned the ladies in this Age of Sensibility.

This was the Golden Age of the master weaver with his indentured apprentices, high wages for his craft and spare time to indulge in self-education and religious and political disputation. The weavers formed the vanguard of the radical Reform and Home Rule movements which flourished in Scotland in the decade following the French Revolution. The United Scotsmen and Friends of the People revolt in 1797 and the Radical Rising in 1820 both required Government spies and force to suppress them. During his Scottish

Above: Detail from a tamboured muslin sampler, Ayrshire, c. 1800. Opposite: William Allan at Jacquard handloom, c. 1885.

tour in 1819 the radical writer William Cobbett answered the weavers' petition to come to the Valley to address them. So fired was he by the commitment of his audience, he wrote, "I would go a thousand miles to see the looks of these Scotchies—especially at Newmilns."

The days of the independent master weaver were numbered, however, as adaptation to the new fabrics led to increased dependence on outsiders for the supply of materials. A class of middlemen, or sma' corks as they were known locally, developed; agents who transported the webs of up to 400 weavers to the Glasgow manufacturers who in turn supplied the agent with the warp yarn and payment to bring back to the artisan weavers. Some weavers actually walked across the muirland path to deal with the Glasgow manufacturers directly but the majority answered the carriers' cry of 'Ocht or nocht fur Glesga' when his cart set off for the city. The corks of course were local men who 'graduated' from weaving stock.

John F. Morton:

"My great, great grandfather had a warehouse, what ye called a wareroom in the old days, and he collected all the handloom cloth and he hauled it on his back or in a barra or whatever into Glasgow. I think he went twice a week and eventually I think he got a horse and cart and took it to Glasgow. But originally he went over the moor. He walked over the moor to Glasgow with the actual bundles o' hand made muslin."

This system was to last throughout the rest of the hand loom period. Despite the decline of hand loom weaving elsewhere, the weavers at work in Newmilns increased from 550 in 1842 to 952 in 1872, while the numbers in Darvel similarly doubled. This was partly due to the successful introduction and adaptation of the Jacquard machine onto the hand looms in 1838 by a local mechanical genius, Joseph Hood. The Jacquard enabled weavers to produce intricate patterns on curtains, table covers and bed covers, products whose very diversity helped the industry to survive. The finesse of the Valley product was able to resist growing competition from machine-made articles throughout the nineteenth century, enabling the weavers to continue in their now quasi-independent state until almost the dawn of the present century. The weavers, however, could not resist market forces and the nineteenth century saw more troughs than booms for the artisan weaver. The mood of the period is expressed in the following examples of local poetry. The first, semi-humorous in vein, refers to the necessity to employ the weavers' children as soon as they are able to walk:

Main Street, Darvel, c. 1880. Handloom weavers outside their cottages.

Chenille Handloom Shop, A. Morton. Darvel, c. 1880.

A weaver said unto his son
The nicht that he was born
My blessings on your curly pow
Ye'll rin for pirns the morn.

The next sums up the frustration of the weaver, thirled to the corks and manufacturers:

Trade it was slack an' wages sma'
An waur than that tae bear.
Agents an' corks in ruthless thraw,
Sought oot each scob and tear.

Doon gaed their glesses on his claith
Whene'er a shot seemed missing.
Wi' stoppages, they werenae laith
His sma' returns tae lessen.

It took the American Civil War and the total embargo on raw cotton which came as a result of it in the 1860s to ring the final knell on the days of the handloom weaver. In the resulting distress many families left the Valley while some turned to the new pits outside Galston for work. The old textile tradition might have died completely if it had not been for the enterprise and vision of one Alexander Morton. The period of transition between the machine lace period and the handloom days was just within living memory in 1981.

John Woodburn:
"Ma grandfather had what they ca'd a two loomed shop and he wis a Galston man, Roxburgh they called him. It wis the staple industry. I mean it wis in my day that, hearin' the handlooms goin' even at night. I remember what they were like right enough jist like a big lace loom on a very small scale—they had shuttles and cards and then they worked them wi' their feet of course—treddles. The women worked the same time as the man, oh aye, that wis a well known fact. At that time there werena the same discipline, they could come off it fur half a day and go up tae the curlin' pond or something like that."

Alexander Morton was himself a weaver of fine madras or 'leno' curtains, who on the death of his brother continued the latter's business as a sma' cork. Up until then curtains were sold to the merchants unbleached and unfinished. By finishing the curtains himself and selling them directly to stores from Glasgow to London, Morton built up a profitable business. It was on one of his selling trips to London that he saw the Nottingham lace machine at work at an industrial exhibition. Despite his failure to convince a majority of the conservative Darvel weavers and agents to help him finance the scheme and bring alternative industry for the declining handlooms, and despite the opposition and reluctance of the Nottingham industry to sell him their looms, Morton succeeded in bringing the first lace machine to Darvel in 1875. Within ten years there were over 100 in the Valley and shortly afterwards Darvel, Newmilns and Galston replaced Nottingham as the world centre of

Interior of lace mill, Newmilns, c. 1900.

the lace furnishing trade. The confidence of the new class of manufacturers in their market for the product is revealed in the fact that by the early 1900s individual Valley firms had opened factories in Barcelona, Oslo, Gothenburg and Columbia, Pennsylvania.

In the Valley a new social order emerged with master and worker on different sides of a widening divide. The alienation of the workers was exacerbated in 1897, when after a long and violent wage strike and

Centre: Building where first power loom was installed, 1875.

lock out, the manufacturers won a hollow victory over the recently organised Newmilns Textile Workers Union. The collective memory of professional strike breakers and imported 'foreign' English blacklegs left the workers with no illusions as to the break-up of the old homogeneous community, and the bitterness remained well after the union was recognised in 1914. The thrawn individuality of the handloom weaver, however, continued on both sides — the manufacturers rarely uniting in association with one another, but determined to dominate the workers, the workers resentful of their loss of liberty and the obvious wealth of the nouveau riche.

Carmichael James:
"They used tae blow the hooters, there's a hooter went at half past six in the mornin' and then it went at nine o'clock for the breakfast; went at twenty-past nine for shift men tae come back in; went at ten o'clock again for them that was away for their breakfast; went at one o'clock, went at two o'clock. Then it went at six o'clock and twenty-past six for the backshift men tae go back in. An uncle in Dervel, he's dead noo, Rab Hamilton, he was a weaver and a tenter tae, I worked beside him. Rab used tae say aboot Dervel, when they were arguing aboot the slaves and that, 'See the darkies, the darkies are wicer than us,' says

1844 1923

ALEXANDER MORTON
WHO LED THIS VALLEY
TO INDUSTRIAL FAME
AND PROSPERITY

The monument to Alexander Morton on the road between Newmilns and Darvel.

he. 'They have to leather the darkies tae their work wi' whips. See here in Dervel, they just blaw a horn and everybody's runnin' tae it.' "

David Drummond:
"They were the meanest lot ever ah seen, ah think, the manufacturers aboot here. They've a' big hooses. One, Alexander Morton, built a big castle there, Gowanbank. This was years ago, before ma time—they asked the men to come oot tae work a Saturday fur him and he would see them alright. He gave them a poke o' readin' sweeties! Ye know, thon sweeties wi' 'I love you' on them—they got a poke o' sweeties each fur their Saturday mornin's work. And then he built a castle! That's true! Tae tell ye the truth we never got naething aff them that we didna work fur."

The 'readin' sweeties' story has perhaps gained in momentum through the generations but it does reveal the 'them and us' attitude which quickly established itself.

Robert Black:
"It was Alexander Morton that brought, you

could say, prosperity here, oh there's no question about that. But he was a hard man too, you know—we'll leave it at that! (laughing)."

John Woodburn:
"He wis of the kind that had tae rule the roost or he wouldna hae naethin' to do wi't. He wisnae an overgenerous man, he was a hard man tae work fur. In 1882 he built Gowanbank and that gave the show away. He showed how much [profit] was in the trade."

Many of the new firms manufactured madras and chenille curtains, in addition to satisfying the insatiable Victorian and Edwardian demand for lace bedspreads, wall hangings, tablecloths and beautifully styled curtains. The Nottingham lace machine was not dissimilar to the Jacquard handloom so the inherent knowledge and skills of the Valley weavers were easily adapted to machine production, while the piece rate system gave the weaver the opportunity and incentive to earn higher wages than anyone else in the factory, thereby helping restore the weaver's pride in his craft in the new environment. The reaction of the worker paid a set wage to the weaver's obsession with output was a mixture of envy and humour.

James Hunter:
"They hated some o' the patterns. They had tae be up and doun the ladders behind their machine, up onto the Jacquards to change cards, reverse them and what have you. One o' the stories when ah started wis one o' the weavers had decided tae take

Detail from the monument, Gowanbank in the background.

a short cut comin' back down and jumped over the front o' the machine and had went over on his ankle. A couple o' men ran over to help him and he says, 'Don't bother with me,' he says, 'get the machine on!' The first week ah started I remember running past this machine and the weaver comin' chargin' after me, cursin' and swearin' — the draught o' me runnin' past him would knock his machine off and interfere wi' his wages! And ah couldna believe this but it turned oot, if there were a door left open, the weavers that were makin' their own pay always came chargin' over and kicked the door and cursed at whoever had dared leave this open tae interfere wi' the machine.

"I remember when I was only fifteen I used tae love tae annoy the old weavers. I would hide behind the machine and you could always watch the rhythm o' the machine and start whistling as if the machine wis squeaking. So the weaver would rush for his oil can and he would oil where he thought the squeak was comin' from. So I just stopped for a minute or two, moved along and started again and it wis guaranteed that he would rush for this oil can, there was no way this machine would get put off for the lack of oil—they always seemed to have an oil can in their hand, the weavers."

Robert Black:
"I was thirteen years of age [c. 1914] . . . you started as a boy at what we called the ravelin' aff—strippin' the bobbins. From that ye went tae the shuttlin', fillin' the shuttles. And then it was the spoollin', [when] a spool is emptied you took it off an' tied a full one on, ye see. You went onto shifts then, ye were what they called a shiftboy. Ye had juist tae learn the loom as ye could. A weaver would say, 'Let me oot for a smoke, Bob', and you would watch the loom till he came back in and you gradually picked it up tae the best o' yer ability, ye see.

"At that time, a weaver nearly had tae die before ye got a chance o' a loom! (laughs) But gradually ye got ontae a machine, an' that was that. Lace weavin' was a job ye were learnin' all the time, you could be years and years in the lace workin' a machine and suddenly you would meet something that you hadn't met with before—there were so many different weaves, single action, double action, Swiss, Madras and comby. If you were on a good machine, it was in good order, you did a good job. In the early days, if the loom wasnae gaun, yer pey wasnae gaun—you only got paid on what ye made. Now a weaver has a guaranteed wage. They can still make extra if the machine's really goin' well, but there is a guaranteed wage. Conditions are better now."

Carmichael James:
"I can go back three generations in ma connections wi' the lace. Ma grandfather came up here frae Nottingham an' he worked wi' Mortons .

. . . I think it would be when the first power looms came. James was his name, Jack James—in fact that was his by-name—English Jack! Ma father was in the lace a' his days. When ma faither wes a schuilboy, he used tae rise early in the mornin' an' gae out wi' ma granfaither an' help him tae shuttle. He came back an' got his breakfast an' went tae the schuil. He cam back fae the schuil an' went back in tae about six o'clock at nicht tae help ma granfaither tae shuttle again. Well, ma faither got nuthin' for that—it went on tae ma granfaither's pey.

"I was the Dux boy o' the schuil . . . but I'd tae go in tae the mull. Ye had tae hae money tae go on [to higher education], so ma faither hadnae the money. Ye juist had tae go tae the mull or the pits. That's hou things went on about here.

"There used tae be a train come in here at twenty-past six in the mornin', an' it was like Hampden Park, about five or six hundred came off it, to work in Darvel. They'd never hae got workers for a' the factories in Darvel. An' I'll tell ye wan thing when I was a boy, the lace weaver would be one o' the best paid workers in Britain. The folk wi' the biggest complaint in the mills was the women. Oh the manufacturers took a rise oot o' them for years—low wages."

Wages in the mills have varied a great deal over the years reflecting usually the market for the product. The fact that there have been few major strikes this century, however, reveals a measured acceptance of wages in the trade. The same acceptance may also be due to the fact that wages were always compounded by

Joseph Hood, pioneer of the Jacquard machine, c. 1870.

Newmilns, c. 1885. The entrance to Joseph Hood & Co. is on the left.

families in which perhaps mother, father, daughter and son all contributed to the weekly household income. In such a unit a small individual pay rise could mean a large increase in income while a prolonged strike could bring immediate economic disaster.

The sense of continuity in weaving from previous centuries to the present day is strengthened by the fact that not a few of the manufacturing class are descended from the original Flemish and Huguenot weavers and that people engaged in the modern industry can speak of direct connections with the hey-day of the handloom period. Such a man is John Hood whose firm still repairs the Valley machines today and whose great-grandfather, Joseph Hood, introduced the Jacquard machine there in the 1830s. Working as he has with the lace machines all his life, Mr Hood has a special admiration for the class of tenters who lie between weaver and manufacturer in the factory hierarchy.

John Hood:

"The tenter was the main man. They were the people that had to put the cloth on the machine and they had to know what the machine could do. You can mention Willie Gold, Davy Lawson, Tommy Rankin, Tommy Morton, Borland, at Stirling and Aulds, Jim Craig, Jim Craig's father . . . they're too numerous tae mention."

James Craig:

"I was what they ca' a tenter. A tenter, when things break doon he's the fellow tae sort it. The job itsel wes interestin' big variety, an' ye'd tae have a guid knowledge o' the trade fae beginnin'

tae the end o' the product. Weavers, oh there were guid weavers, there were some weavers that werenae just sae hot, and there were ithers that just didnae seem tae cotton on tae it. The guid weaver wes worth his weight in gold tae ye."

The lace looms were manned twenty-four hours a day by three shifts of workers. The weaver's insistence on keeping his machine going even precluded the usual lunch break.

Alec Black:

"I used tae carry a can an' a piece tae ma faither. He sat at the en' o' the loom an' et his piece. Nou, tae keep the tea warm we used tae go an' put it on top o' the safety valve in the boilerhouse an' when

Tapestry weaving, c. 1900. The tenter is on the right.

Derval Dam

Medium

It happened on a Lammas Nicht As I gaed oot for a stroll I

had nae gone sae ve—ry faur Tae I daunered doon by the Toll. I

daunered on an' daunered on Tae Derval Dam I did pass And

wha dae ye think was staun-in' there But a bonnie wee servant lass.

CHORUS

Whaur a'e gaun, gie me yer haun' How dae ye do, says I, Haud

up yer heid ma bonnie wee lass, And din—nae luk sae shy.

Whaur dae ye bide? Whaur dae ye stey? Come tell tae me yer name. Will yer

faither no be ang—ry noo If I wis tae see ye hame?

We stood a while an' crackit
  About a thing or twa
We werenae thinking o' the time
  Tae the staurs gaed a' awa'.
She drew her shawl aboot her heid
  And solemnly did exclaim,
Says she, 'Young man, ye'll keep yer word,
  Ye promised tae see me hame.'

And noo that we are merrit,
  And happy as can be,
Wi' twa wee bairnies by oor side
  And anither yin on oor knee,
We'll sit aroon our ain fireside,
  And talk o' days gaun past,
But I'll ne'er forget that nicht I met
  Ma bonnie wee servant lass.

Mills and bleachworks on the Irvine from the southern slope of the Valley, c. 1890.

he wanted his tea he sent me down tae the engine man tae get it."

Carmichael James:
"Somebody came up wi' yer hot piece and yer can o' tea an' ye just sat by your loom an' ate it—tane in the black lead an' everythin'. An awfu' durty job, the lace, awfu' durty."

Robert Black:
"When ye left the factory, ye wis as black as the ace o' spades. That lead that they use for the combs, ye see they can't use oil where the shuttle runs . . . it's black lead, like graphite [they use]. Ye was polished like a black man.'

Fortunately the factory workers could balance their hours in the hubbub of the factories with time spent in the peaceful beauty of the surrounding countryside.

Carmichael James:
"I've seen us in shifts, in the guid weather in the summer, five or six o' us, we used tae feenish at twa an' hurry an' get away up the watter tae swim. And in the backshift, ye wes droppin' [finishing the shift] at eleven. Instead o' gaein' hame an' washin' yersel . . . ye went hame, lifted a towel an' a bit soap an' went doun tae the Irvine—a guid summer's nicht . . . did that . . . oh it used tae be great! Did a lot o' things in the countryside. Walking was a great thing. Then in the spring ye went fur peeser's [peewit's eggs], in the autumn ye went fur rasps.

There wes a place up there ye'd fill a basket ony time. We used tae rake the countryside—roun' the ferms an' liftit the eggs for the fermer . . . but he didnae haund them intae him. (laughs)"

By the 1920s and '30s the factories had established their own work rituals and practices, the humour of which was often directed against young apprentices. The latter had to suffer horseplay and indignity in order to be accepted into mill society.

Carmichael James:
"It was a custom when a boy stertit in the mull, the women got a haud o' ye, ken . . . yer private parts—used tae rin, but they got ye—that wis you in the lace then! Then when ye were boys ye got sent a' the daft messages if ye wis stupit enough tae go. Ye were sent for left-haunded screwdrivers, or a pail o' steam, or . . . 'Awa' ben there an' tell the warper tae gie ye a long staun [stand]!'
"If ye wes a guid riser, ye got the keys an' opened the mull in the mornin'—maybe got hauf-a-crown for it. Well ye maybe opened a swing door, an' afore ye even got the light on, the first thing that met ye wis a big pot or a big ba' o' black lead—hit ye richt in the face gaun in in the mornin'. Did it no' mak a mess o' ye! The backshift left it fae the nicht afore.
"There wis ae fella used tae get the gaffer's watter ready tae wash his haunds at droppin' time. So this nicht the gaffer gaes ower an, 'Oh ya,' he says, 'ye've aboot burnt the haunds aff us. Whit the

hell . . . did ye no' pit ony cauld watter in it?' 'Aye,' says the fella, 'the cauld watter's at the bottom.' (laughs) He wis some man that.''

Alec Black:
"This weaver made a mistake, he had made an awfu' long darn. He wis sent for to the Gray

Hand darner. Newmilns, 1982.

Room [where they check the lace for faults] an' he said tae the Gray Room foreman, 'It's no' possible for me tae hae a long darn . . . I never hiv long darns!' The foreman says, 'Well, ye've just walked through ane, we hung it over the door!' ''

The Greige (or Gray) Room staff are mainly women whose job it is to repair and finish the piece.

Mrs James:
"I startit when I wis fourteen. I went tae whit ye ca'ed the measurin' o' the cloth. Efter, ye got a step up, an' ye went tae the drawin' tae look for the faults. Ye wis there for aboot a year then ye went tae the dernin'. Well, ye got six weeks tae learn the hand dernin'. Ye could either be a machine derner or a haun derner. But when they got a machine, there's nane o' them wad leave so ye just had tae gae tae the haun dernin'.
"It was an auld Mrs Glen that learned me. Ye got dernin' everythin'—spools, shuttles, holes, great big derns wi' maybe six row oot o' them. Well, ye had tae learn tae pit a' that in the pattern. See the like o' that flower there [indicating a lace table cover], well if there were a bit missin' in that flower ye had tae sit an' dern it so's that it would be the full flower. Ye were never coontit skilled.''

One of the reasons for Alexander Morton's original success with his leno curtains was the importance he placed on good design. The survival of the lace trade is partly due to the beauty of those Victorian designs and the continuation of a line of designers such as John F. Morton, who could adapt the tradition to suit modern taste. The sudden death of Mr Morton in 1981 weakened one of the pillars of the Valley trade.

John F. Morton:
"My faither an' mither were both designers—ma faither was wi' ma grandfather in Holland in 1912—he was a tenter and they were building a new factory. My wife's grandfather, he set up a factory in Sweden. But this is the only place now that makes lace to any extent.
"We do the designing which is drawing freehand and then it goes to this squared paper. The colours are a code for the [Jacquard] card cutting people, and they cut the cards according to what we put on the paper. We are commissioned to do these designs by local factories, by factories in Nottingham, Spain, Austria and India. Every country has a different idea of design—characters; swans, angels, floral, old-fashioned, Victoriana, modern.
"There's one manufacturer, he 'phoned me here an' told me tae come up to one of the local bars. I went away up wi' the umbrella over the head and it was really comin' down, bucketin' down an' he was standin' outside in all the rain, quite inebriated. Now they had just newly whitewashed the wall [of the pub] and the rain was trickling down over the wee parapet at the bottom o' the wall. Says he,

Darvel Lace Queen Jean Murdoch (Paton) with procession, 1953.

'Right, that's what I want ye tae draw!' We had that as a design an' this is whit ye had tae draw, rivulets running over the parapet o' the wall! A character!''

The effect of the industry was not confined to the factories. The Valley towns were always recognised by outsiders for the beauty of their window decorations, due to the range of local curtains available to them. During the 1930s and the 1950s a day was set aside during Darvel Fair holidays for the crowning of a Lace Queen, a day on which to show off the beauty of the staple industry.

Robert Black:
"You come intae Darvel at the bottom end there and honestly you could hardly see a building for lace . . . lace curtains draped in practically every house in the village—fantastic!''

Morag Ritchie:
"At the time I was Lace Queen I worked in a sample department . . . I still work in an office in a lace factory. Each lace factory was asked to nominate two employees who had to be resident in Darvel and unmarried. The firm I worked in had some new designs and I was allowed to choose a design and the dresses were made locally. I'll never forget the thrill . . . and I'll never forget seeing a sea of faces . . . to me it looked like ten thousand people. A lot of people, mostly I think with Valley connections would come back. It was a day that families got together. I think the town has lost a lot by this bein' dropped.''

Piano puncher interprets design pattern on Jacquard cards.

Lace weaver. Newmilns, 1982.

As the Lace Queen festival died so the very existence of lace came under threat in the slumps which followed the boom years experienced by all textile manufacturers during and in the years immediately following the Second World War. In the 1960s I.C.I.'s synthetic terylene fabric, with its lightness and drip-dry properties, appealed to the housewife more than the more expensive and less convenient lace product. Many factories changed over to terylene production. It was a change received with ambivalent feelings by the work force.

Jim Hunter:
"The lace weavers reckoned there was no skill [in it] . . . just a wee boy's job watchin' the terylene machines. They used tae laugh, called them toys, 'Are ye watchin' the wee toys?'"

Carmichael James:
"You went this wey tae yer work, clean as anythin'. It was an' awfu' easy job. Ye see ye'd only a warper, a weaver an' changers. There were nae darnin' wi't, nae mendin', nae shuttlin', nane o' that. Ye maybe watched fower [machines] . . . maybe twa or three o' these wadnae stop a' shift."

Most of the factories which did not buy terylene weaving machines went out of business. The shrewdest manufacturers who maintained diversity in their production were rewarded with the demand for dress lace which was fashionable in the 'swinging '60s'.

J. F. Morton:
"Durin' the boom o' the 'sixties we did a table cover for a local firm. The next time we saw the cover it had a Mary Quant label on it! It was for a poncho—she had cut out a hole in the middle and put a zip on it . . . two holes for the arms and that was it. I don't know what it would be sold at but it would be more expensive than what it would be sold as a lace table cover, that's for sure!"

Jim Hunter:
"They were workin' night and day for months and months, twenty-four hours a day, just tae get this dress material oot. They were sellin' no' jist yards . . . miles tae America. It was in a' the big magazines . . . models wi' it in *Vogue*. It was supposed to be the world beater but like all other things it jist came to an end."

The liquidation of numerous lace firms in the decade following 1955 resulted in many lace machines being sold abroad, thus opening up future competition for the Valley product. Those firms which survive in Newmilns and Darvel today make mainly terylene and lace nappery. Whereas the trend was towards cheaper synthetic goods in the '60s, today it is the firms exploiting the specialist luxury end of the market who have more reason to be confident about the future.

Mitchell Allan:
"There are eleven firms in the Valley making lace. We see the lace going on and on provided we keep our old machines in good condition and provided we keep tabs with the market. We've concentrated our markets in Europe using the old traditional skills and designs that this industry had and this firm kept since 1881."

Ironically, it is a return to an older fabric in the Valley's textile history, silk, which is helping Mr Allan's firm, Haddow, Aird and Crerar, retain its work force. The chance survival of Madras looms in Morton, Young & Borland of Newmilns not only provides that firm with a good American market but gives the industry a direct link with the muslin curtain handloom weavers of the nineteenth century.

Morton Dewar:
"During the late 1950s and early '60s the cotton

Young Newmilns Madras weaver, 1982.

weaving industry was in severe decline and many of the companies took advantage of the Government's scheme which enabled them to scrap looms and receive payment for doing this. We nearly closed our Madras department but just at the time that closure seemed inevitable, orders started to come through from America . . . and these have continued to this time."

The last major slump in the staple industry of the Valley fortunately coincided with the rise of employment opportunities in the engineering factories of Kilmarnock. Now in the 1980s we have witnessed the collapse of that town's prosperity with the withdrawal of Massey Ferguson and the resultant increase in the ranks of the unemployed along the banks of the Irvine. Many Valley mills are on short time with several facing possible closure. Now more than ever it is to be hoped that imagination in marketing can be allied to the skills of the weavers to guarantee a future for this unique traditional industry and its beautiful products.

Hope for the future is based on examination of the past, which has given this experienced tenter faith in the manufacturers' ability to endure.

James Craig:
"They've gone through a' their bad times, they survived. They started away wi' the old lace curtain, they got on tae coloured cord an' silk, and when that began tae go, they startit anither thing— the terylene. And they're still in it, they're still survivin'. It's the history o' the lace trade—they're survivors."

BILLY KAY

Notes on Contributors

BILLY KAY was born in Galston, Ayrshire, 1951. Producer, B.B.C. Scotland, Radio Drama. Has published poetry in *Made in Scotland*, editor Robert Garioch (Carcanet Press) and short stories. Edited *The Edinburgh Pub Guide* (E.U.S.P.B., 1975) and *Odyssey–Voices from Scotland's Recent Past* (Polygon Books, 1980). Recorded Robert Fergusson's poetry and music on 'Fergusson's Auld Reikie' (Iona IR003). Originator and producer of Odyssey for Radio Scotland.

MURDOCH RODGERS was born in Glasgow in 1950. He is a postgraduate student at the University of Edinburgh. Author of 'The Lanarkshire Lithuanians' in *Odyssey–Voices from Scotland's Recent Past* and 'The Anglo-Russian Military Convention of 1917 and the Lanarkshire Lithuanians' in the journal *Immigrants and Minorities* (March 1982).

IAN MacDOUGALL was born and brought up in Edinburgh. Staff tutor in History and Trade Union Studies at Newbattle Abbey Adult College. Published *Militant Miners* (Polygon, 1981), *Essays on Scottish Labour History* (John Donald, 1978). Honorary Secretary, Scottish Labour History Society. Presently compiling a Pictorial History of Labour in Scotland.

MARGARET BOCHEL is a primary teacher and local councillor in Nairn. Member of Nairn Fishertown Museum Committee. Published *Dear Gremista* and *Nairn Fishertown Weddings* (with the support of County Life Archive, National Museum of Antiquities). Currently working on *The Fishertown of Nairn*.

IAIN FRASER GRIGOR was born 1949 in Morar. Studied at Strathclyde and Glasgow Universities. Works as fisherman, freelance journalist and broadcaster. Published *Mightier than a Lord* (Acair, 1979), the story of Highland land agitation, and wrote 'The Seven Men of Knoydart' for *Odyssey–Voices from Scotland's Recent Past*. Contributor to the *Glasgow Herald* and *Sunday Standard*.

ISHBEL MACLEAN was born in Edinburgh, 1948, brought up in Plockton and Skye. Producer, B.B.C.Schools Radio. Wrote 'Mountain Men' for *Odyssey–Voices from Scotland's Recent Past*. Produced the Odyssey programmes 'Mountain Men' and 'The Pearl Fishers' for Radio Scotland.

LORNA LEWIS was born in Thurso, Caithness, where she worked as a newspaper reporter and features writer. Moving to Ayrshire, she headed an oral history project based on the lives of Glengarnock steelworkers. Now edits and produces a staff magazine for an Edinburgh department store.

BILLY ROSS was born Glasgow 1954. Studied Scottish History at Glasgow University. Professional musician with Ossian for four years. Founder member of Crannachan Folk Band.

ELSPETH KING was born and educated in Fife. Curator of the People's Palace, Glasgow's Museum of Local History, since 1974. Author of *The Scottish Woman's Suffrage Movement* (People's Palace, 1978) and *Scotland, Sober and Free, The Temperance Movement 1929-1979* (People's Palace, 1979).

Further Reading

Billy Kay (Ed.), *Odyssey–Voices from Scotland's Recent Past* (Polygon Books, 1981). Raphael Samuel (Ed.), *People's History and Socialist Theory* (Routledge and Kegan Paul, 1981). Paul Thompson, *The Voice of the Past: Oral History* (Oxford University Press, 1978). School of Scottish Studies, *Tocher* (quarterly journal). E. J. Cowan (Ed.), *The People's Past* (Polygon Books, 1980). J. M. M. McPhail, *The Clydebank Blitz* (Clydebank Town Council, 1974). *The Clydebank Blitz in Pictures* (Clydebank District Libraries, 1980). U. Marin, *Italiani in Gran Bretagna* (Centro Studio Emigrazione, Roma, 1975). R. Page Arnott, *The History of the Scottish Miners* (Allen and Unwin, 1955). Margaret Bochel (see above). William Stewart, *A History of Fishing from Stotfield, Seatown and Branderburgh from the Year 1500 to the Present Day* (C.R.N.M.D.S.F., Lossiemouth). *Fishing in Scotland from the Sixteenth Century to the Present Day* (Lossie Printers). Malcolm Gray, *The Fishing Industries of Scotland, 1790-1914* (University of Aberdeen by O.U.P., 1978). Alan

Moorhead, *Gallipoli* (Hamish Hamilton, London, 1956). G. F. Kunz and C. H. Stevenson, *The* ̇ ̇
(Macmillan, 1908). Betsy Whyte, *The Yellow on the Broom* (W. & R. Chambers, 1979). The tapes and trans ̇ ̇
Glengarnock Project are lodged with B.S.C. Archives, Glasgow. A. J. Youngson, *After the '45* (E ̇
University Press, 1973). W. C. Mackenzie, *A History of the Outer Hebrides* (Alexander Gibson, 1903). Elspeth Kn ̇
above). Brian Harrison, *Drink and the Victorians, England 1815-1872* (1971). Ian MacDougall (see above). A. Le ̇
Origins of Glasgow Jewry (Glasgow, 1947). James Mair, *The Origins and Establishment of the Machine Lace Industry in
Ayrshire* (M.Litt. Thesis, Glasgow University, 1973). Alex G. McLeod, *The Book of Old Darvel*; John Woodburn, *A
History of Darvel* (both Walker & Connell, Darvel). The Scottish Oral History Group publishes a newsletter, *By Word
of Mouth*, available from the Honorary Secretary, Iain Flett, Archive and Record Centre, City Chambers, Dundee,
DD1 3BY. The Scottish Labour History Society have published *A Catalogue of Some Labour Records in Scotland* (1978),
available from 21 Liberton Brae, EH16 6AQ.

Acknowledgements

The editor would like to acknowledge a special debt of gratitude to all those interviewed for Odyssey: without
your contribution the series and books would not exist. Thank you for your time, kindness and hospitality. I wish to
thank the authors of the individual chapters for their selfless work on the book's and programme's behalf; Gavin
Sprott and the staff of the Country Life Archive, National Museum of Antiquities, Edinburgh, for their help in
processing the photographs; Stewart Conn, Head of Drama, Radio, for his sensitive guidance and support for the
Odyssey project; Christopher Irwin, Head of Radio, Scotland, for allowing access to B.B.C. resources in the
compilation of this book and for his promotion of the series.

THE CLYDEBANK BLITZ
Photographs: Clydebank District Libraries (thanks to Pat Malcolm).
Thanks to Gerard Boyle for contacts.

ITALIANI IN SCOZZIA
Photographs: *The Glasgow Herald.*
Yerbury Galleries, Mrs M. McGillivray, Mrs E. Di Ciacca,
Mr F. Pontiero.

MUNGO MACKAY & THE GREEN TABLE
Photographs: Scottish Record Office.
Lodge St Mary's, Newbattle.
James Reid, Mr Yuill, David Spence.

THE FISHER LASSIES
Photographs: Margaret Bochel.
Country Life Archive, National Museum of Antiquities.
Thanks to Ron Grant for contacts.

Song: 'The Herrin' Shoals' was written and performed for the
radio programme by Ian Sinclair of Mirk and Caledonia.

GALLIPOLI
Photographs: Imperial War Museum.
B.B.C. Hulton Picture Library.
Ian Boughton, John Brown, Mary Kate McKinnon.

THE PEARL FISHERS
Photographs: Country Life Archive, National Museum of Antiquities.
Scotland's Magazine.
A. & G. Cairncross Ltd.
Betsy Whyte, William Moodie, William Elder.
Poem: Sheila Douglas.

GLENGARNOCK STEEL

Photographs:
Mrs A. Munro, Mr Joe Smith, Stephen Ruxton, Mr John Dempsey, Miss Maggie Bell, John Lewis.

The original material for 'Glengarnock Steel' came from a Manpower Services Commission Project, sponsored by Cunningham District Council, British Steel Corporation and the S.D.A.

CLAN NEIL OF BARRA

Photographs:
Mary Kate McKinnon, Nan McKinnon, Barbara MacDermott.

Songs:
The singing of Flora McNeil.

Thanks to Paul MacInnes, Morag MacLeod and Anne Cullen for assistance with the Gaelic.

THE '26

Photographs:
National Library.
John McArthur, William Murray, A. Wilson, Mrs Thomson, the Misses Proudfoot.

GLASGOW JEWRY

Photographs:
City Archives, Glasgow.
B.B.C. Hulton Picture Library.
Dr J. Miller, Mrs Woolfson, Mr M. Tobias, Mr P. Brooks and Ms J. Brooks.
Mrs Nyren (née Geneen).
Mr James Gillies (People's Palace).

Song:
The Mitchell Library, from *The Hebrew Anthology of English Verse*, Ed. Ruben Avinoam (Tel Aviv, 1956).

WHISKY'S AWA'?

Poster and Photographs:
People's Palace Museum, Glasgow.
B. Aspinwell, University of Glasgow.

UP THE VALLEY

Photographs:
James Mair, Victor Albrow, Norman Chalmers, Joseph Hood & Co., Newmilns; Haddow, Aird & Crerar, Newmilns; Morton, Young & Borland, Newmilns; National Museum of Antiquities; Jean Paton, Robert Black, and Fleming & Co.

My thanks to Jim Hunter for contacts and James Mair of Newmilns for his excellent thesis on the lace industry.

I would like to extend personal thanks to Norman Chalmers for taking responsibility for the music and photographs; Murdoch Rodgers for his advice and tireless co-operation; my secretary, Joan Raffan, for painstaking transcription and organisation; all who proof-read the articles and helped in the book's production, including Jamie, Mary, Sarah and my wife Joáo; Stewart Conn for points of style; Jim Hutcheson for the cover and logo; the staff of Polygon Books, Margaret, Neville, Mary and Pam, and in particular Adam Griffin for his accuracy in typesetting, and Nigel Billen for his commitment to the book and his skill and patience with the layout and design.

BILLY KAY